I SWEAR

Janet Cahill

POOLBEG

Published 2006
by Poolbeg Press Ltd
123 Grange Hill, Baldoyle
Dublin 13, Ireland
E-mail: poolbeg@poolbeg.com
www.poolbeg.com

© Janet Cahill 2006

Copyright for typesetting, layout, design
© Poolbeg Press Ltd

13 5 7 9 10 8 6 4 2

A catalogue record for this book is available from the British Library.

ISBN 1-84223-265-7
ISBN 1-84223-265-1 (From Jan 2007)

Typeset by Patricia Hope in Sabon 11.5/15
Printed by Creative Print & Design, Wales

About the author

Janet Cahill was born in 1968 in inner city Dublin.

At times a difficult place to navigate, Janet survived the pitfalls that most embraced. Despite all the odds, she travelled the world, settling in North America for seventeen years. Previous occupations include waitressing, childcare and cleaning. She has now found writing an outlet for her emotions.

Inspired by her mother and friends to write her experiences, she has written *I Swear* to highlight the issue of addiction and its effect on everyone it touches.

She now lives in Dublin with her son.

Acknowledgements

Writing these acknowledgements meant a lot to me and they come from the bottom of my heart.

The best place to start is with my ma and da. Every word that describes good people describes the two of you. You are the best parents in the world.

Lynn, without you my friends and family would not have me around. You gave me my life back and brought the old Jenna back to life. Never a day goes by that I don't think of you.

My family: Davy, thanks for always being so kind to me; Diane, what can I say but your door was always open and there was always a dinner on the table; James, you're a great brother and brilliant on the other end of the phone when I need a man's opinion; Miriam, to this day seeing you always makes me so happy and you always manage to put a smile on my face; Gerard, I'm glad I got to know you better when you stopped off from your world tour to visit me in America – it was great to have you around; Gavin, ah Gavin, you're the best and when I need you, you are always there; Granny, thanks for just being the best granny in the world; Aunt Jenny, thanks for believing in me and thanks to all the aunts and uncles, cousins, nieces and nephews.

Thanks so much to the people who made this book possible. My editor, Anne O'Sullivan: without Anne there would be no book. Anne, thanks for always believing in this book from day one. You helped build my confidence up and like Lynn brought me to where I am today. To all at Poolbeg Press: Paula and Kieran. Kieran, I remember the day you said to me "We'll take care of your baby". I thought that was so funny. By the way, the book *is* my baby. Thanks also to Claire, Niamh and Lynda.

Thank you, Robert, for all your help with the computer and thanks to Julie McDaniel. We had great nights working on the book in my ma's house. Thanks to Gerry O'Callaghan and Joe Costello. Colm Keane, thanks for the Urban Plunge. Thanks to Cyprian Brady. Thanks to Stephen MacDonagh for the grammar and to Sandra Mara for the advice.

Thanks also to the Taoiseach Bertie Ahern for the quote.

Anita, thanks for always being there. A big thank you to all my great friends who have been with me all of the way; especially Maureen, Caroline, Linda and Pamela, Rhonda, Mary and Paddy Cahill and family and Jean, Roger and family. Thanks also to all my friends and neighbours in America, Baldoyle and Balrothery. Thanks to all the staff at Rutland Street School and to all of my past teachers. Carol and Helena, it's great to have you back in our lives.

I want to say to all of you that through the darkest days of my life over the last couple of years you have all stuck by Jonathan and me and those memories will stay with me forever. I love you all. Thanks a million for everything.

For my son Jonathan

Prologue

Before I ever thought of writing a book I was in a friend's house in Boston one day, just standing in the kitchen, when I happened to look at her fridge and I saw this lovely saying. I thought about it for a while and about how relevant it was to my life and how it had turned out. That day I promised myself that if I ever wrote a book I would start with the following lines.

OUR LIFE IS A BOOK OF CHAPTERS THREE:
THE PAST, THE PRESENT, AND THE YET-TO-BE.
THE PAST IS GONE, IT IS STOWED AWAY;
THE PRESENT WE LIVE WITH EVERY DAY;
THE FUTURE IS NOT FOR US TO SEE,
IT IS LOCKED AWAY AND GOD HOLDS THE
KEY.

Well, here are some chapters from my life . . .

1

My name is Janet Cahill, or Jenna as I am called by everyone, and I grew up in Dublin in the 70s in the inner city. We were a big happy family even though we were quite poor. It was hard to make something of your life where we grew up but lots of people did and I am lucky enough to be one of them. Though I have to tell you even when I was a little girl I knew that I would make something of my life. Of course, I had no idea just what that was going to be, but I got there and I have to say that despite lots of things it was mainly because of the great family I have. And in one sense this book is also their story. We were close then and today we are all still close and always there for one another. Looking back I suppose I was a very determined girl but for all of us it was my mother, Martha, who was our real inspiration. She lost a lot of her family to drugs but she was determined that the lives of her children would be different so I took after her. She is such a strong person and everything we do even today has her mark on it. I could all have gone the way of so many young people growing up in the inner city but I didn't and if this book shows anything it shows that life is about the choices you make for yourself and that we are all responsible for our own behaviour. This is what we heard every day in our house. Our ma believed in all of us and believed that we could all have good lives. And, of course, she was always giving us lectures as kids and those lectures usually ended with the same statement:

"You can be anything you want to be in this life. It does not matter where you come from; it's the person you are that counts."

But for some people where you came from did count. All around us people were getting into trouble with the police and up to no good. In Dublin in the late 70s drugs were starting to take a grip. Unlike today there was no information or help available to educate young people about the dangers of drug abuse and addiction. You were on your own and whether you survived or died was down to the choice you made for your own life. Nearly every family I knew in the inner city around where we lived was affected by drugs.

And they were starting to die. Young addicts died leaving heartbroken families absolutely helpless. And in many cases the parents of these young people were left to look after and rear the children left behind. Many of the relationships that these children were born into were not stable in the first place as both parents were often addicts and unable to look after themselves let alone the babies they were bringing into the world.

Grandparents or brothers and sisters took the children into their own families and reared them as their own. In the midst of their addiction many of these poor people tried to warn others, like myself, of how dangerous drugs were. It was too late for many of them but they tried to save their families and friends from the suffering and inevitable death that lay in store. From the youngest person caught up in the drug scene to the now desperate young criminals dealing on the streets and in the flats, none foresaw the way their lives would turn out. Sick, addicted, dying and lost, these people inhabited a city in the grip of poverty, huge unemployment and prejudice. The inner city was experiencing rapid population decline and in a survey carried out in the Sean MacDermott Street area in 1981, the results showed that out of a population of 8,000 only twenty adults and fifty teenagers were employed in manufacturing industry. The city had been stripped of industry, leaving these areas which had previously relied on low-skilled jobs devastated. Dublin overall was changing as a capital and all new office space was concentrated outside the city leaving a decaying capital behind. Few completed their education and without opportunity or support the young people were left to their own devices to make life on the street their career. The only way to survive was to adapt to the situation quickly and accept your lot. Those who did survive did so only because of the love and support of a strongly united community where people looked out for one another. While one week it could be a neighbour's child in trouble, next week it could be one of your own. Week in and week out more and more kids lost hope, and in despair sought refuge in heroin addiction. Whereas before the late 70s and early 80s, crime in the inner city was related to poverty and boredom, now hordes of young people opted out of their society and communities and became heroin addicts. From then on small-time addicts became big-time-strung-out junkies and had to find ways of feeding their habit. Of course, the only way to do this was through thieving and robbing. The statistics were frightening, with the north inner city where I was born experiencing a bigger drug problem than the Harlem district of New York. Drugs and Aids were something we associated with American television programmes and now we had a bigger problem. Statistics are all very fine for me to talk about now but when I was a kid it wasn't about statistics and I wouldn't have understood them anyway. But what I did understand was what I saw happening to my family and friends. An aunt, uncle, parent or child is not a statistic when you are burying them. They are precious loved ones leaving great sorrow behind. And for me the greatest tragedy of all was the damage that the drug-pushers were doing to their own communities. They were killing their own by selling drugs to the people they were living side by side with so that they in turn could feed their own addiction. But I don't think they knew that when they sold drugs to their friends and neighbours they were handing out death sentences. At that time neither the Garda nor the government were able to get a handle on the scale of the problem. Yes, crime was on the increase in the inner city and they went all out to deal with that. They arrested the addicts for shoplifting and for robbing cars and handbags. All they could do was take them off the streets but nobody had yet stopped to look beyond the crime to the petty, pathetic addicted criminals who were making the crime-lords superwealthy.

But in the middle of all of this there was my family and lots of families just like mine. We loved our homes and our neighbours. We all lived close to one another and I suppose what kept a lot of us going was laughter, love and the strong sense of community that existed in the inner city.

This story is the story of my life, a story of hope and inspiration, of dreams shattered and lives rebuilt. I fulfilled most of my dreams and, yes, going to America was one of them. From growing up in inner city Dublin with holidays in Sunshine House and Butlins to the white sandy beaches of Aruba in the Caribbean, my dream of seeing the world was fulfilled. I believe my hope brought my dreams to reality and when my life hit rock bottom it brought me back up again. But then again life always throws in a few surprises and for me writing this book was the greatest one. As my marriage crumbled I began to write my story and that writing brought me back to my childhood and the strong roots it gave me. I found those roots again. My story is not one of misery and deprivation. It is a simple story showing that, though life can be very hard to endure from time to time, you can pick yourself up and get going again and make a good life for yourself even if everything is not perfect.

2

St Joseph's Mansions, 1982; My brother James who was twelve at the time and our cousin Vanessa who was thirteen were taking care of my Aunt Jenny's kids. Aunt Jenny was my ma's sister and one of her children, Gavin, was handicapped and in a wheelchair. He was a lovely little guy and everybody wanted to make him happy. The only holidays our family, or anybody else who lived around us, knew at that time was a week in Sunshine House in Balbriggan in north County Dublin or the annual trip to Mosney, or Butlins as we called it. Only kids were allowed to go to Sunshine House but the whole family, adults, everyone, went to Butlins. Butlins meant freedom and laughter and fun. Anyway James and Vanessa had a brainwave. They decided to bring little Gavin and the other kids to Butlins for the day, but the only problem was that they never told anyone where they were going. Well, they were excited and everyone was laughing and joking and it just slipped their minds. They headed down to Connolly Station and hopped on a train. When they arrived at Butlins they found an empty chalet and decided to stay overnight and give the kids a bit of fun. When they got hungry, James and Vanessa brought all the kids over to the restaurant. (When you went to Butlins on your holidays, you paid for full board and that included all of your meals.) Well anyway, off they went and thought to themselves that if they were stopped they would say that their mother would be with them shortly. Now while they were having a great time in Butlins everyone in Dublin was worried sick, thinking about the worst that could happen. My ma was in work that day in Matt Kelly's furniture shop down in Mary Street when my sister Diane came to tell her the news. James had been staying with my granny for the weekend so my ma thought that he was safe. A search was mounted and all of the places that they might go were checked out. Gavin's uncle, headed down to Butlins but he didn't spot them and went home again to break the bad news to the whole gang back in Dublin. There were no mobile phones then and they had been missing for a whole day and night at this stage.

The *Evening Herald* newspaper was called and a plea went out to the public from the police to come forward if they could be of any help or if they had spotted the kids anywhere. Poor Jenny was crying to my ma, *'Martha, you only have one kid gone, I have three.'* She cried her heart out. But whether she had one child gone missing or three it didn't matter to my ma. Her child was missing and she was in a state. All through the night the search continued. But you don't just lose seven kids in the city so Gavin's uncle still had a strong feeling that they had gone to Butlins and headed back down for another look. When he walked into the big hall in Butlins there were James and Vanessa sitting playing bingo. Vanessa had won a flask already and was hoping to repeat her luck. They had put the kids in the nursery for a few hours so they had been responsible as far as they were concerned. Everyone was so delighted and relieved to see them and the story made the front page the next day in *The Irish Times* under the headline 'Seven go for a day at camp'. My ma went to Connolly Station to meet them the next day and the platform was filled with reporters from radio, television and all the newspapers. She was expecting to see the kids looking dirty but, not only were they okay, they were spotless. Vanessa had washed all the kids' clothes and had given them baths. You know, Butlins was almost like our second home because we were brought there so much so they were quite happy there and felt very safe. They had put their families through hell but their hearts were in the right place as they wanted to do something special for the kids. And, thank God there was a happy ending to that story. This was the funny, mad, sometimes wild but always loving environment in which I grew up.

* * *

But let me start at rock bottom. On the 18th of March 2003 at about 10.30pm I was at home with my son Jonathan when I got the worst phone call of my life. My husband, who was at that time in America, called me to tell me that our marriage, was over. After eighteen years of being together I just could not believe it. I was completely shocked. Yes, I guess we had problems but, you know, nothing that couldn't be solved I thought. The next day I bought two tickets to America, to plead with him not to give up on his wife and child. When Jonathan and I arrived in Boston on the evening of the 20th March, Paul was not around. When we called him he was home within minutes and I could tell by his face that he was angry and not very happy to see us. We stayed for a week and lived together as a family but it didn't convince Paul to stay with us. Within a couple of days of our arrival Paul wanted us all to leave Boston and go to Cape Cod. I didn't understand why he wanted us to go away but I agreed. Deep in my heart I felt that he was running away from something or that he didn't want me to see something. Honestly, I thought that he might be having an affair and that he had something to hide. I had no proof though and when I asked him he denied it. I tried to talk to him but we just could not communicate. He was, of course, polite to me but so very distant. Sometimes he was the same man I had fallen in love with and then suddenly he would seem cold and distant. I found it very hard to handle so I wrote him a letter explaining how I felt and that no matter what decision he made I hoped he would be a big part of Jonathan's life always. Paul later told me that he read the letter every day and that it meant a lot to him. We headed to Cape Cod to the Irish Village where we had spent many family weekends. It was almost like a little bit of Butlins that I felt I was passing on to Jonathan. I spent most of that weekend in tears as I wanted to be with this man so much. I was heartbroken but Paul seemed to be clear in his mind that it was over between us. We had been together, since we were sixteen so this to me was unbelievable. I thought we had been through so much together, growing up in Dublin and moving to America to make the wonderful life that we had together.

I will never forget one night when we were all in our hotel room and Jonathan was asleep I was so distraught that life as I knew and loved it was over that I just ran from the hotel and down the road as far as it would take me. It was the middle of the night and the streets were empty. Really I didn't know what I was doing but I just knew I had to keep running. I was lost in the world at that moment and I just stood in the middle of the road crying and looking up to the sky for God to help me. The odd car passed me and beeped its horn but I didn't care what happened to me that night because as far as I was concerned my life had ended. I was convinced that he had found someone else, someone who could make him happy as my depression had made me so sad for a number of years. I made it back to the room that night and eventually fell asleep. The next day, with my head in a different world and not on what was once my family, we headed down to the beach for a walk with the dog. It was nice for us all to be together like that but deep in my heart I knew that it was the end of those family times together. We headed back to Boston and, with no hope left, we had to leave. Before we returned to Ireland the three of us had a family hug. Then Paul hugged me. Of course, I was crying my heart out. I asked him if our marriage was over. He said it was not but somehow I really didn't believe him. I guess deep in my heart I knew.

* * *

Back in Dublin I still could not really believe that it was over. I convinced myself that Jonathan and I would be heading back to Boston when he finished school in July and that everything would be okay. A few weeks later Paul returned to Ireland so that we could all go on holiday. At this stage I was absolutely terrified at the thought of seeing Paul, not because I was afraid of him but because the pain and hurt were unbelievable. No words can do justice to how I felt at that time. I couldn't eat or sleep. I was surviving on about four hours' sleep each night. Only for my family, friends and neighbours I don't think I would have got through this. They helped me take care of Jonathan because he too was going through so much. You know, I just couldn't understand it. To think he had a daddy who loved him so much and who meant the world to him, and yet now he was no longer going to be part of his everyday life, that's what hurt me the most and to this day I don't think anything or anybody could ever hurt me as much again. It was like a death. I really didn't want to be around any more if I was the problem because then I thought they would have each other. The thing that meant more to me than anything else in this world was their relationship with each other. When Paul came home to Ireland, he and I went down to one of the local pubs. I was so nervous I could hardly breathe as we just sat in complete silence. I didn't want to hear those words 'IT'S OVER'. Oh, my God, those words just terrified me, but I knew they were coming.

"Paul," I said, "what about you and me?"
"There's no me and you any more, Jenna."

There are no words to describe how I felt at that moment but I know in hindsight that I really felt deep inside that Paul was letting go and deep in his heart he really didn't want to, but I guess I was wrong. There was nothing I could do.

* * *

Jonathan and I made one last trip to America but Paul packed his bags and left us. We now had to rebuild our lives alone. Would that be in America or Ireland? It was, of course, Ireland where we had roots and history and family.

3

So I better go back to the beginning to tell you where I grew up and all about my family. The best place to start is with my granda and granny because they laid down the foundations of our family and to understand my life growing up in the inner city you have to know a bit about them. So here it goes.

What you are about to read in this chapter is not very nice so it's up to you if you want to skip it or not but I think it will give you a little understanding of what type of father my ma grew up with and my granny had to live with. And it will show you just how strong these two women are still to this day. My granda was born in 1923 and grew up on Drumcondra Road on the north side of the city with his grandmother while his mother and father lived in St Mary's Mansions in town in a two-bedroom flat with their other fifteen kids. When he was about fourteen he went back to live with his mother and father but the move was no good for him and he started to mitch from school and to steal. He was caught and sent to an institution in Kerry a long way from home for a young Dublin fella He was brutally treated in this place as the priests seemed to believe that as he grew up the only way to make him behave was to beat him into it. The abuse was both mental and physical and his life from here on out was filled with violence. When he was sixteen he met my granny, Elizabeth Burke, who on the other hand had grown up in a very happy home environment just a few blocks away from my granddad in Avondale Flats off Cumberland Street.

My granny and granddad dated for a while and then got married. Together they had nine kids one of whom died at birth. My granddad brought the violence and abuse that had been beaten into him in Kerry into his own family after he got married. Little did my granny know what she was getting herself into. Their first home was on North Great George's Street in Dublin's north inner city and it wasn't long after they got married that my Granny experienced my granddad's temper first-hand. One day her niece bought some cakes for my granddad for his tea but because he didn't like them he made my granny and the young girl walk around the courtyard of the flats six times and say sorry.

At that time most babies were born at home and just hours after my granny had given birth to their son Bimbo, my granddad came home looking for his dinner. Of course, she didn't have it ready so in a fit of rage he lifted up the washing machine and threw it at her and she had to be brought to hospital because of her injuries. One of the midwives from the Rotunda Hospital was with my granny at the time and witnessed the whole thing. Charges were pressed against him and he was sentenced to six months in prison but this was just one of many violent attacks against my granny. They moved a couple of times during the early years of their marriage but eventually they ended up in a flat in St Joseph's Mansions where they lived together with their children for thirty years. One by one the kids got married and left. He was generous with his money and gave all of his children enough money to set up their first homes. But all the time he remained very abusive, not only to his wife but also to his kids right throughout his life. One time when the Beatles were all the rage, one of his sons, B-Bob, was mad to have their hairstyle and had his hair styled in the same way. Of course, my granddad didn't approve and told him to get it cut. When he arrived home after the pub that night, B-Bob was in bed and my granddad noticed that he hadn't got his hair cut. In anger he took the poker from the open coal fire and hit him over the head, leaving him with twenty-six stitches. Poor B-Bob woke to find his blood all over the bed. After these attacks of violence granddad showed no remorse and just went on as if nothing had happened until he was ready to lash out again. He would come home drunk every night and then you could be sure that the night would end with a fight. From time to time he would get so out of control that he would break every piece of furniture in the flat. Of course, for the next couple of days after leaving the police station, he would feel guilty and give my granny the money to go out and furnish the whole house again. He was never short of money and

Janet Cahill

never left my granny short. He had a good patch parking
cars and he made plenty of money at it. As a matter of
fact my ma always says that the only good thing about
him was that he was generous and he would even give her
friends the money to go to dances. And they always had
the best of clothes. Now granddad was good with a
sewing machine and when Davy Crocket-style hats were
in fashion he made them for all the kids in the flats. But
he could be very brutal the next minute. One particular
night my ma was on a date with my da and she was
supposed to be home by eleven o'clock. She was late by
about five minutes and he beat her up, leaving her with a
broken arm that time. I know my ma says that he was
good with money but what the hell is all that worth when
you have no family life? But he was her da so I suppose
she wants to remember his good points.

He used to drink in the same pub as the Dubliners and
they all used to go back to my granny's flat from time to
time. His drinking pals only saw the good side of him. He
was a street angel and a house devil. My granny used to
say to him,

"Gem, would you please stop drinking?"

He would always give the same reply

*"Will you tell me how I can get from O'Connell Street
to St. Joseph's Mansions without passing a pub?"*

Sometimes he would listen to the priest and take the
pledge for six months and be the best but still they had to
be on their guard. There was only one priest that he
would listen to and that priest would come and give him
the pledge in the hope that it would stop him drinking.
But it never did!

One night when my granddad came home drunk the police had to be called yet again. When they knew whose flat they were going to they never came alone. At least eight policemen would come at one time all lined up one by one on the stairs just waiting for the right moment to get him. On one occasion he put a chain around my granny's neck and tied it around the door. He called out to them, *"If you open the door she will die."* Another time he got a gas bottle and threw it over the balcony of the flat at one of his sons. I tell you he didn't care. People used to say that even the police were afraid of him. He hated when young fellas came screeching into the flats in their robbed cars at night and would get into a rage and chase them out. They were afraid of him too and would run for their lives. My granny remembers very well the day he gave her money to buy new clothes. She wore them that night and, of course, she felt beautiful and hoped that this would be the end of all the fighting. But, as soon as she arrived home, he ripped the clothes off her back in anger and took the scissors to her beautiful long black hair. What a life to live! And what a legacy to leave!

But like anybody I suppose he wasn't all bad. St Joseph's Mansions were the only flats around town that the fire brigade couldn't get into because of the gates. One year a flat went on fire over on C Block and my granddad had to throw a bike through the window to rescue two members of the family. He saved their lives but tragically two other members of the family perished. While their flat was being redecorated their neighbours took the family in and helped them out until they got back on their feet again. My granddad had no respect for anyone because he had never been treated with respect when he was growing up. And the tragedy of it all was that my granda's death was caused by a violent act in which he was the victim. He was out one night and soon after leaving the pub he was found down a lane unconscious. He had been beaten up and robbed. He was brought to the Richmond Hospital where they had to operate on him while the police made yet another visit to their flat, this time to break the bad news of his attack to my granny. While the doctors were operating however, they discovered a hairline fracture to his skull going back many, many years. The doctors later asked the family if he suffered mood swings over the years. The family started to wonder if this was why he was such a violent man and so brutal and angry to his wife and kids and many other people. They reckoned that this fracture probably happened while he was in the home in Kerry as he received so many beatings down there. When he finally got out of hospital he had to travel from home to St Vincent's Hospital for a long time. He eventually deteriorated so much that my granny had to put him into a home on the Navan Road. She was getting on and wasn't able to look after him and he died in the nursing home of heart failure soon after. Whenever she went to visit him granny got very upset; even though he was bad to her and his children for all those years she still didn't like to see him suffer. She no longer blames him for everything that happened over the years. She believes that the way he was treated as a young boy in Kerry made him into the violent man he became.

My ma was only fifteen when she first fell pregnant for my da, who was only seventeen at the time. My granda made her get married but as she was too young to be married in Ireland she was sent to England. So off they went over to my da's brother-in-law, and my poor ma didn't even know them. She had no choice. So they married and then she gave birth to her first baby boy in June of that year. She was only sixteen at this time. Their early marriage was spent in England where my da found good work painting and decorating while my ma reared the kids. I always feel very proud of my ma and da and all they do for the family but I am especially proud of the fact that my da saved a man from drowning.

During their time living in England my da went by boat to visit his sister in Wales. On the boat journey a man jumped into the water and my da noticed him going over the side and jumped in after him. This made headline news in the English and Irish papers and the Queen awarded my da a certificate. Unfortunately my da was working at the time and had lied about his age so that he could get more money. So when the Queen was looking for him he was afraid to go forward in case he got into trouble so they sent the certificate by post later. He still has it to this day.

Da grew up on Killester Avenue on the north side of Dublin, one of a family of ten kids. There were five boys and five girls in the family and he was the youngest so he was spoilt rotten. We didn't really spend a lot of time with my da's family but there was one brother that we were close to as he worked alongside my da. Paddy and my da are like twins and when I'm around Paddy I don't miss my da as he reminds me of him. My ma also came from a big family of four girls and five boys but we spent a lot of time with them because we all lived in the same flats.

4

And now to my childhood . . .

I grew up in 11B St. Joseph's Mansions on Killarney Street in the inner city. I had three brothers, two sisters, no bathtub, telephone or car. I remember everything about my childhood, back even to before I made my First Holy Communion. Growing up in the flats was real living. We lived in a world of our own with all of our cousins and close friends living in the flats right beside each other. I could stand out on our balcony and shout and someone would always come out and answer me and the chances were that it would be one of my cousins. There were four blocks in our flats: A block, B block, C block and D block. My Granny Burke, my ma's mother, lived on A block with her husband, Gem. Beside her and just a few doors away lived my Aunt Mary, my granny's sister-in-law, and her husband, Skinner, and their eight kids.

Underneath them lived the Crosbeys. That was my

granny's brother and his family. They had eight kids. My other Aunt Mary lived on the other side of my granny with her two children. My ma and da and all of us kids lived on B Block and a few doors away lived my ma's best friend, Jean, her husband, Roger and their two kids. Two doors away from them lived my Aunt Jenny, her husband, Neddy, and their three kids.

My Uncle B-Bob lived on C Block. I don't know why we called him B-Bob (since he lived on C block) and he had three kids but only two of them lived with him. His other little girl lived with her mother in England. The Fowlers lived on D Block. This was my granny's sister's family. She lived there with her husband, Ned, and their six kids. Wouldn't you think we lived in a prison the way I talk about the blocks? But you know we had FREEDOM and a lot of it!

My ma had six children while we were living in St Joseph's Mansions. There was Davy, he was the eldest and a wild kid most of the time. He lived with my granny on A Block and we never saw that much of him but the one memory I have of Davy was of his pigeons and, boy, he had lots of them. His pigeon loft was the pram shed down in the yard and while he spent most of the day looking after them I guess they kept him out of trouble. Diane was born next. The eldest girl, she was a great help to my ma and also became my ma's best friend. As the eldest girl my ma confided in her a lot but if there is one thing we all remember about Diane is that she was terribly accident-prone. One year she was knocked down on Parnell Street by a car and ended up in Cappagh Hospital for weeks.

This accident left her with one leg half an inch shorter than the other. And then shortly after she was walking on a wall over in Sean Tracey's Flats behind St Joseph's Mansions when she fell off and broke her other leg. My da always called her 'Hop along Cassidy'. Ah, there was always something wrong with Diane but she was beautiful and the fellas were always after her. One after the other they never stopped coming to call on her and sometimes I envied her.

Then there was me. I guess I was a little bit wild in my own way but deep down I was kind-hearted and I was always thinking of others and how I could help them. From a very young age I was very ambitious and independent and never liked to ask my ma and da for money. I suppose this was my business brain developing even at a young age.

Miriam was next to be born and I tell you she was just gas and always made us laugh. Miriam was never really confident and I used to feel that for her. I wished at times that she could have had half my confidence but, all the same, everyone loved Miriam. She always had a smile on her face and just wanted to be happy. Then there was James. James was a very good-looking fella and had all the girls after him. To be honest James and I didn't always hit it off too well as kids. I suppose like all brothers and sisters growing up we sparked off one another a bit, but now we're best friends.

The last one of us kids to be born at St. Joey's was Gerard. He was the apple of our eyes and we called him 'forty winks' because he hardly ever slept. Then later on in years my ma had what she always called the 'shakin's of the bag' – Gavin. We all doted on Gavin; he was our baby and the best kid of all. So as you can see there was a big gang of us all living together in that flat and, yes, sometimes I guess it was tough but most of the time it was great. Everyone looked out for each other and helped each other along. Oh, by the way, I nearly forgot. We did have a late arrival to our family, our cousin Sharon. She was B-Bob's daughter and when she came home from England at the age of fourteen my ma took her in to live with us. Sharon spoke with an English accent which made her a bit exotic in St Joseph's Mansions but she was really nice and very popular with everyone. She was mad and was always game for any bit of fun so she fitted in well with Diane. Sometimes Diane, Miriam and Sharon and a bunch of fellas would be in St. Mary's Mansions down in Sean MacDermott Street and at night-time they would jump over the balconies on to the concrete ground below. It was a game to them but, when Sharon decided to join in with them one night, she jumped over the balcony and broke her leg. They all ended up in hospital with her that night but that was nothing strange when we were growing up as someone was always being brought to Temple Street Hospital with some injury or another.

* * *

The people living in the flats took great pride in their homes and my ma was no different and had our home like a palace. Let me bring you on a tour of our little palace. Our flat, 11B, was on the first floor. It was a corner flat with a big balcony and to us it was very private because nobody needed to walk past our flat to get to their own place. We had a beautiful mahogany hall door and, as you entered the hall, immediately to the left there was the toilet. Now the toilet consisted of a toilet bowl with a big cistern high up on the wall and a long chain hanging down. There was no handbasin in any of the flats in those days and having only one toilet was most of the time terrible and sometimes very funny especially when everyone wanted to use the toilet at once. The worst time would be when we would all be rushing to get ready to go to school in the morning or when we were playing down in the yard and had to run up to go to the toilet. Someone would always be in there and you would be dancing outside shouting, *"Quick, quick, it's coming."* Of course, whoever was in the toilet would be laughing their heads off thinking it was so funny.

A little further along the hall just before the sitting-room and to the right was the first bedroom. We called it the 'bedroom on the balcony' and it was the smallest bedroom in the flat but it was not that small at all. We were able to fit a double bed in it which still left a good bit of walking space around it. I remember my ma had that wood-effect beauty board that was everywhere at the time lining the walls of the bedroom. But, Jesus, I remember too that that room was always very damp. Every winter's day my ma would declare that you would catch pneumonia in it. I was always sick as a child so I was never put in that bedroom. On down the hall was the sitting-room. It was big, bright and beautiful and my ma always had it done up really nicely with wallpaper on the walls and beauty board over the fireplace. There were three big windows that brought lots of sunlight into the room. The floor was covered with lino and it had a leather couch that my ma, for some reason, called the 'grandfather suite'. There was a little coffee table in the middle of the floor and I remember well that table being put up on the couch every day so that the floor could be swept and washed. My ma was scrupulous or as the women in the flats would say years ago, 'scoopless'. Even the windows had to be kept spotless all the time and the white lace curtains had to be really white. My ma used to buy her curtains in Guiney's in Talbot Street where all Dublin people did their shopping. We got new curtains once or twice a year and they were washed every time the windows were cleaned which was every other week. We never had an open fire in the flats because my ma thought they were dirty and the idea of having to clean it out every day would be a pain. We had an electric fire but we also had a gas fire that was moved around the flat to warm it up. I remember my ma or da would put it into our bedroom to warm it up before we went into bed. This made the whole place cosy and I always felt warm and safe as a child growing up in that flat. My ma had lots of brass ornaments on the mantelpiece. She loved her brasses especially one she had in the shape of three little monkeys, one with his hands over his eyes, one with his hands over his ears and the other with his hands over his mouth. My ma would look at them and would say to us, "*See no evil, hear no evil and speak no evil.*" And when she and her friends would be talking adult talk she would point to it and say, "*Children should be seen and not heard. Just like those monkeys.*"

Pride of place over the fireplace went to a picture of a boy with two tear drops coming from his eyes. It was a nice picture but I used to feel sorry for that little boy crying and often wondered why he was crying. Off the sitting-room was the scullery which was a very small room with a sliding door leading into it and presses lining both walls. There was just enough room for a cooker and a small fridge. (Though I remember milk and bread were bought every day. As a matter of fact even to this day, in my ma's house, bread will not be eaten if it is even only a day old.) Now because the scullery was so small my ma had a piece of wood that she used for a table hinged on to the wall. When we had dinner we sat at it and when dinner was over my ma cleaned it and then it was put down flat so that the scullery would look a little bigger again. The sink was under the window overlooking the front of the flats. That room was very small; ah, sure you wouldn't swing a cat around in it. We had no immersion heater back then so the only way to heat water was on the gas stove. But while we had water we had no bathtub, so when it was bath time in the house the plastic or tin bath was pulled out and pots of hot water were poured in. All of us kids were washed in this tub, two at a time and then it would be refilled for the next two.

But you know what? We didn't know any better so bath time was always fun for us and felt cosy, and that's what mattered. Off the sitting-room was a big bedroom with a window running to the front and another window facing the back of the flats. All of us girls slept in this room and, with the daylight flooding in, it was really bright on a nice sunny day and it had a veranda to the front and another at the back. Our cousins lived on A Block so their bedroom was side by side with ours and we shared both verandas. This was great for when we wanted to play 'nick-nack 'against their window at night. Now that didn't happen that much, because their da was kind of strict so you wouldn't dare mess that much. However, if we ever heard an argument going on in their flat we would get a glass and put it against the wall to try and hear what was going on. Sometimes it was funny and we got a great laugh. The rows would have to be loud though because in the flats the walls were made of concrete so it was quite hard to hear. Off the other side of the sitting-room and to the right of that was my ma and da's bedroom. With just three bedrooms there was no room for arguing over who slept where. The girls shared one room and the boys had the other. One of the many things I really loved about the flats was that when you walked through the front gate you would see the women cleaning the brass knockers, and hanging out their washing or just scrubbing their front steps. I felt that I was part of one huge family and it gave me a lovely warm feeling all over. And all of us kids who lived in the flats played together and went everywhere together just as brothers and sisters would in a big family. Nobody was ever left out of a game no matter what age they were, the more the merrier. We stuck together and looked out for one another. And it wasn't only our home that my ma took great pride in; she was very proud of all of her children. Whenever we went out we were always immaculately dressed and when we were little kids my ma never stopped buying us clothes. I remember once actually telling her to stop buying us new clothes as we didn't need any more. But she would just say that she liked to have us all dressed nicely. I thought she dressed us all very nicely and we just didn't need new clothes every day.

But there was no talking to her so I just decided to say no more. As I got older my ma would give me the money to go up town and buy my own clothes. I remember sometimes I would say that I hadn't seen anything that I liked and I would just give her the money back.

* * *

From birth to death the people in the flats always came together to help one another. When you walked in the front gate of the flats you would know immediately if someone had died. A white card would be tied onto the gate with the name of the person who had died nicely printed on it. And within a day or two of the death two ladies would go around the whole four blocks and collect money to help the family with the burial. Now it was very important to show respect for the dead at that time but I remember sometimes we would go around to the morgue on Sheriff Street or the dead house as we called it, where we would try to sneak a look at a dead person. I swear we got into so much trouble because for some reason we always burst out laughing: a mixture of nerves, sheer fright and immaturity, I suppose. Sometimes we would just have to run out and one of the older ones would give us a dig.

"Stop laughing. That's terrible, laughing at the dead."

But we laughed at the way that adults would talk about the dead. They took mourning very seriously back then. They would be dressed head to toe in their best black. There they would be standing and, of course, most of them with a cigarette hanging out of their mouths.

"Did you ever see a corpse like it? Isn't she beautiful?"

"God, I have never seen a corpse like it."

I often wondered did they mean this or were they trying to make the family feel better? But, now years later and even to this day, even though my Aunt Betty is ten years dead, they still talk about her and say how she looked like a porcelain doll. She was beautiful and when she died they put the best make-up on her so that she looked even more beautiful.

5

Now writing about poor Betty brings me back to when drugs started taking hold in the inner city. I was around nine or ten at the time so I was old enough to be aware of what was going on. My ma had two sisters and a brother on drugs. I remember being in my granny's flat one day and when I walked into the scullery I saw my Aunt Betty standing there injecting drugs into her arm. I knew she was on drugs but this was the first time that I actually witnessed it. Poor Betty was only eighteen years old. I watched as she put a string around her arm to make the top part of her arm firm, to get the vein to stand out. There was another person with her and they helped each other. I guess it made it easier for the needle to go in. She was surprised to see me standing looking at her but she just reacted very calmly and said, *"Jenna, don't ever do this 'cause what I'm doing is very wrong."*

I know that I was very thankful to her for her telling me

that but to be honest she didn't have to tell me because I knew what I saw that day wasn't at all good. But I was very sorry for her. This was my first time ever to see anyone injecting themselves but it wasn't to be my last. Before drugs came into our area you could run and play anywhere in the flats but later as the problem grew we heard of people injecting on the stairs and asking for vinegar to sterilise their needles because they were sharing needles. It hurt so much to hear this but, thank God, I was strong and decided never to take drugs. I think one of the reasons I stayed out of trouble was that my ma always said to us before we went out the door every day, *"You don't have to do what your friends do."*

She always said this because she knew that sometimes the older girls in our gang would be puffing cigarettes on the stairs so she knew there were temptations to do stuff that was no good for you. The older ones always smoked on the stairs or in the broken-down pram shed so that they wouldn't get caught. I had a puff once or twice but I never really liked it. I remember one girl would say to the other, *"Go on try it. It's great."* Then another one would say, *"Jesus, you're not inhaling it right."*

And then you would hear an adult coming along and the girls would have to hide the cigarette behind their backs or up their sleeves and you would hear a shout of, *"Fuck that bleeding cigarette; it's after burning my bleeding hand."* Before you went home you would have to eat chewing gum to get the smell of smoke off your breath. We would smell each other's breath to make sure the smell of the cigarette was gone but we forgot that our ma could smell it off our clothes. I tell you we were right old ones altogether and pretty innocent considering what was going on all around us. I suppose we thought we were more grown-up when we smoked.

* * *

But life in the flats changed when drugs took over. My ma was very aware of the terrible damage that drugs were doing to her sisters and brothers and was very determined that her own kids would not get caught up in the drugs scene. She could see first-hand that drugs in the inner city at that time were killing off an entire generation of young people and nobody seemed to care. It was as if the inner city was just an ugly sore that should be covered with a useless bandage and not treated. Nobody wanted to talk about drugs and nobody wanted to see the poor addicts who were dying off. I suppose the police were helpless really but they could not ignore it forever. We could see the increase in crime happening before our very eyes every day as we walked to and from school. One day Anita, my first cousin, and I were walking down Killarney Street which was a very busy street with a lot of traffic. As we were waiting to cross the road at the traffic lights we heard the sound of glass breaking. A young fella had smashed a car window and robbed a woman's handbag. Anita and I ran over to her and asked her was she all right. We told her to wait while we ran into the flats to try to get her bag back. We were disgusted by what we saw and we tried to find her bag but, it was too late. The kids would take the money really quickly and throw the bag down the rubbish chute so it was impossible to find. We went back to the lady and told her we couldn't find it even though we had tried but she was very upset. This happened every minute of the day to loads of motorists brave enough to drive down that street and the police had no hope of catching these lads because they all dyed their hair the same colour and wore the same style and colour clothes. The young people on drugs would do anything they could to get money to feed their habit and smashing a car window was no bother to them and an easy way to get cash.

And at night you would hear robbed cars being driven around the flats at high speed. The screech would be so loud that it would wake you up and you would hear the lads shouting to each other, *"Here's the cops"*, and then they would run for their lives. I tell you sometimes they would climb the roof of the flats to get away and other nights the robbed cars would be burned out in the courtyards of the flats when they were finished screeching around the place in them. I used to be so mad at this because I knew that someone had worked very hard to buy that car. This happened several times a week. Around this time, 1980, life in the flats changed and started to get very bad. Many of the mothers and fathers were really upset with what was happening and they decided to start up vigilante groups. They would sit at the gates at night and monitor who entered the flats in an effort to put a stop to the crime. It worked for a while but then it went downhill again. The people just gave up and eventually started to move out. That's when my ma decided to go over to the corporation to try to get a new house. She wanted so much to move from the city centre to the out-skirts of Dublin to get us away from the drugs that were taking over St Joseph's

Mansions. Whenever a flat became vacant, the addicts and pushers would move in and squat in it. Then it became known as a good dealing spot and people came from all around to buy their fix. Not only did my ma want to move but every day of the week you would hear the women in the flats talking about moving out of the city. They couldn't do anything about the ones who had died but now they wanted to move on with their lives and make a better life for their young children before they got caught up in it as well.

Nearly every family in the flats had lost at least one member of their family whether it was a child, niece, nephew, or even a mother or father, to drugs. Before drugs really hit the inner city badly we heard only of the old dying. When drugs started to take their toll, then all you would hear was of the young dying.

My ma eventually got a new house in Baldoyle and I swear it was like winning the Lotto, she was just so happy. I will never forget going out to see the house for the first time. It was brilliant. All of us kids were just running around the whole house saying,

"Jesus, look, Ma, at the size of the garden."
"Ma, look, there's an upstairs in here."
"Ma, look, there's even a bathtub."

This was just great. I was very happy but, a little sad leaving the inner city. We moved out of the flats around 1981.

* * *

The first year that we lived in Baldoyle my da didn't live with us. My ma and da had separated, so apart from getting a new house it wasn't a great year at all in our lives. We were living all over the place. I lived in Anita's house for all of that year because I missed the city too much. My sister Miriam lived with my other cousin and to be honest I don't know where everyone else lived. Some of the time my ma stayed in my Uncle Bimbo's flat in Ballybough close to the city when she hadn't got enough money to get the bus into town every day to go to her job in Mary Street. I stayed there some nights and I tell you it wasn't good at all. I remember walking in to the sitting room to see my uncle injecting a needle into his toes. His veins were wrecked from drugs and this was the only place he could get a needle in. I had seen enough of this to put me off drugs for a lifetime and I didn't want to see any more. I never told my ma about any of these incidents because I knew she would be very upset, and that she would worry. She had enough tragedy in her life without worrying about us following into that drug scene. But she didn't need to have any worries about me as I knew from an early age that drugs weren't for me and as well as that I always listened to my ma and what she said meant more to me than anything else. I knew she was talking from a wealth of experience and that she had seen enough in her life to be able to talk and give advice about the right and wrong way to go in life. She is the strongest person I know and how she survived what happened to her sisters and brother shows just how strong she is.

* * *

My ma's sisters, Mary and Betty, and their brother, Bimbo

were very close in age and were always together. My granny would still say that the reason they turned to drugs was because of the way their da treated them. But my ma says that it was the friends that they were with at the time. Whatever the reason, drugs destroyed their lives.

Mary was mad funny and wild altogether but like me she was very strong-minded so I don't know why she turned to drugs. I think the crowd she hung around with probably played a big part. She started on drugs by smoking hash in the early days and from there she got onto harder and more addictive drugs.

Like Mary it was the friends that Betty hung around with that led her to using drugs. Now, I am not saying that it was the fault of the friends because you have to have your own mind and do what you think is right and not just follow the crowd but some kids are stronger than others and able to stand out against the crowd. If you did not feel strong enough or have the confidence and there was all this smoking hash and shooting up going on around you, then you could get caught up in it and find yourself with a problem. Well, Betty's boyfriend was on drugs at the same time. Unlike Mary, you never knew when Betty was around because she was so quiet. Betty was beautiful and kind and gentle and we all called her 'Betty Blue Eyes'. Everybody loved Betty. Anyway, no matter what the reason was that they turned to drugs and no matter how nice they were they had to feed their habit and that was the only important thing in their daily lives. And how did they feed their habit? Well they robbed almost every day to get stuff to sell for drugs. They would rob mainly from the big department stores in town such as Dunnes Stores and Switzers (now Brown Thomas) on Grafton Street. In their own peculiar way they felt they weren't robbing the poor people and that the shop owners could always claim money back from their insurance so that made it okay. They actually hated robbing and Mary would say to me, *"Well, what else can you do when you're so sick? It's no harm to rob the rich, especially when we help the poor."*

Now when Mary said that they helped the poor what she really meant was that when they stole the clothes they would come back to the flats and sell them around the doors. I swear I would be shocked at the stuff they used to get up to at times. But, you know it was just the way of life in the flats even though you knew it was wrong. But what could you do as a child? They would get us kids to go around the flats and sell the clothes for them and then they would pay us a pound for our work. I never liked to do this because I knew it was wrong and if you were caught by the police you would get into trouble for handling stolen goods. But I tell you, you would not dare say no because you would be afraid. I was especially afraid of Mary because she always got around you in a certain way. She would say to me, *"Jenna, you sell all these for me and I'll get you something. You see. I'll surprise you."*

And, of course, I would give in. But I tell you I never liked doing it because I knew the clothes had been robbed. Again I knew I was doing the wrong thing but there was no way out. And when I got a bit older I got into big trouble with her because I spoke my mind and said, 'No!' They weren't that smart though and after a while the security guards got to know them. Then they would have to disguise themselves. Mary was funny and even in the hard times she had a good sense of humour. She would dress up as a nun or as an old lady to go into town robbing.

One time my granny was sick and called for the doctor. When he was leaving Mary asked him for a lift to collect her cleaning. Out of the car she hopped and went into Switzers and robbed a few suits. The doctor was waiting around the corner for her in the car. She thanked him for the lift but she was laughing behind his back at the same time. It was a horrible thing to do but people on drugs don't do very nice things. When they went off out in the morning they would say that they were going to work and they would come in the door in the afternoon saying they were exhausted. They would be out from morning until night and they really saw it as work. Sometimes they hired a taxi to do the driving around for them but mostly Bimbo did the driving. When it got to the stage where every security guard down Henry Street and Grafton Street knew them, no matter which way they were dressed they had to go further afield. They travelled all around Ireland like a bunch of movie gangsters with Bimbo at the wheel of the car. In later years I learned that many of the security guards took pity on them. I spoke to one man who had been a security guard in town for over 35 years and he said that he would stop them at the door because he knew what they were going to be up to in the shop but at the same time he had pity for them and actually liked them a little. They had a peculiar set of morals; they had no problem stealing to buy drugs but when it came to their kid's First Holy Communion or Confirmation they wouldn't dream of stealing clothes. If one of them told him on the door that they had a child for Holy Communion or Confirmation he would let them into the shop to do their shopping because they would not dream of stealing clothes for that. That would be wrong and against their code of morals. They weren't bad people and they were doing themselves more harm than any of the people they ever robbed from. Now Mary hated giving her money to the drug-pushers. One time they gave her a load of drugs to sell for them. Well, Mary went missing and the drug-pushers came up to my granny's door and my granda chased after them and told them to leave his kids alone.

* * *

And then they started to die. The first of my ma's family to die was her sister Mary. Mary had three kids and when she was very bad on drugs she went to England. My Granny reared two of their kids while the youngest stayed with Mary in England. But because she was on drugs her son was taken from her and given up for adoption. She was a very good-looking girl with big blue eyes, long eyelashes, blond hair, high cheekbones and a figure to die for. Despite all her troubles Mary loved to write and she had a real talent for it. My ma has kept everything she ever wrote so that Mary's children can read it if they want to. You always knew where you stood with Mary because she was very outspoken and direct. She married once but that only lasted six months.

I remember one day she showed me her arm and I swear it looked like a cross had been cut into it. God, it was a horrible sight. She told me it was an abscess and that sometimes worms crawled out of it. I'm not too sure if she was telling the truth about the worms but I know that she was trying to turn me off drugs.

One day my granny got a phone call from England to say that Mary had died. We were all devastated. It was hard on my granny and on my ma and her sisters, particularly because of the way she died and the fact that she was a young woman only in her thirties. An abscess on her arm became infected and she had to go into hospital to have it removed. When she was given the anaesthetic she went into cardiac arrest and died. The drugs had weakened her body over the years and her heart had given up. My ma and her best friend, Jean, had to go over and identify the body. It was very hard for my ma but she would do it than allow my granny to. When my ma saw what Mary's apartment was like she just had to run outside. She couldn't believe that her sister, who had been once so house-proud, had ended her days in such a place. All Mary was left with in that apartment was a Bible and a ring with one diamond; two diamonds were missing. My ma was devastated to think that drugs had ended her life this way. When ma told Mary's husband, Pat McCormack, the news he just collapsed on the ground as he loved her to bits. My ma had to go to see him because she had to find out if their marriage had been annulled. She needed this information for the death certificate. Later my ma, Jean and my cousin Vanessa, B-Bob's daughter headed back to Mary's apartment to get Mary ready. They knew she had to be brought back to Dublin to be laid out so they wanted her to look her best considering no one had seen her in a long time. So they picked out a nice outfit and Vanessa tried it on and lay down on the ground pretending to be dead, so that way they could see how Mary would look. Jean told Vanessa to close her hands and join them together, so that they could see how she would look.

"Ah yeah, she will look gorgeous in that, Martha."

"Yeah, she will do, Jean. That will be lovely."

Vanessa started to laugh when she realised what she was doing and with that they all started to laugh. In the end they brought the body home but my ma found it hard to recognise the body as it was so badly affected. So nobody got to see Mary. This was hard for my ma to tell my granny. For a long time after that my granny felt that she had never buried her daughter. She still thought she was alive and at times she would wait for her to walk in the door. My ma would say, *"Mammy, it was Mary."*

"Ah, Martha, how do you know because you didn't see her."

All of Mary's boyfriends over the years, the fathers of her children and even her ex-husband were at her funeral. She was loved so much. The fathers still have contact with their sons today and I know that they have a good relationship with them. This would have made Mary very happy because she loved her children.

Betty was the next to die. She was also on drugs and they were to ruin her life too. When she became ill she hadn't the strength to fight her illness. You see not all addicts died of overdoses but drugs racked their bodies and greatly weakened them. After giving birth to her youngest daughter, Roslyn, the doctors told Betty that they had discovered cancer cells. Before she was told about her cancer Betty was on drugs. She used to go on and off drugs at different stages. When she was given an appointment for the hospital, being so busy with four kids she ignored all the letters. Four years later she got pregnant again and when she had her scan the doctor told her that she had a tumour on her womb and advised her to terminate the pregnancy. Betty didn't believe in abortion and went ahead with the pregnancy. At five months she had another scan and the doctors told her she was going to have a boy. She was over the moon at the news as this was her first boy after four girls but she had to have a Caesarean section at six months. Because she was so ill the hospital gave her a private room and just a few days later when my ma walked into the room Betty was out of the bed washing the floor. My ma said to her, *"Betty, what are you doing out of that bed, washing those floors?"*

"Martha, I can't lie in dirt. It's bad enough being in hospital without being in dirt also."

I tell you even on her death-bed Betty was scrupulously clean. She was funny sometimes because when she wasn't in hospital cleaning she would be at home cleaning. I used to die laughing when Betty would get the kids to get out the window after washing the sitting-room floor because she didn't want them walking across her clean floor. When she got the news about the tumour on her womb she had to go to St Luke's Hospital for treatment. They would send a bus to St Mary's Mansions to pick her up and she would tell the bus driver to wait until she had finished washing her floor out. That was the best I ever heard. I swear no matter how sick she was she would never let the place go. She had that flat like a palace. She lived for her home and kids and they all even had to have new clothes and they were dressed beautifully every day. Betty had to have a lot of treatment at Luke's. They started her on chemotherapy treatment then she had to have radiotherapy which she called having 'the bulbs'. She was in a lot of pain but my ma always said to her that the doctors were going to make her better. At this stage my ma knew there was no hope. Before all the treatment started, Betty knew she wasn't well and she went to see the doctor. The doctor told her that she had only weeks to live and recommended that she find someone to take her kids. Betty came out to my ma straight away and told her the news but my ma said to her not to listen to the doctors. *"Who are they to say when you are going to die? Only God knows that. Don't listen to them."*

My ma was devastated but Betty just said to her, *"Martha, I want only you to take my kids."*

Of course, my ma said yes. This was a very sad time in all of our lives. I prefer to remember Betty the way she was when she was well and not at the last stages of her life. She suffered a lot. The drugs and the cancer had wrecked her body but she was a fighter and fought hard to stay alive for her kids. My ma did her best to make her comfortable but she got worse by the day. Jenny had all of Betty's kids in her house at this stage. I know that everyone suffered very badly watching Betty going through this pain but it was hardest for the kids who were losing their mother. In spite of everything, anyone that knew Betty knew that she was a brilliant mother. Betty's poor kids didn't just lose their mother but they lost their father also. Only months after Betty's death he stopped contacting his kids and this hit them very hard. The oldest of Betty's kids, Leonda, was only fourteen when she lost her beautiful mother. Nicola was nine, Carly seven, Roslyn, five and Alan only six months old. My ma and da were, and still are, just great to those kids and they give them the best life that they can. I remember one time when I was coming home from America on holidays and my ma asked me to get toys for the kids. She wanted them to have everything because they had lost their ma and she was always trying to make them happy. This particular year I was coming home from America for my da's fiftieth birthday party. It was November and I came home on my own. With things being cheaper in America I brought everything home. Now my ma gave me the money and, thank God, I kept all the receipts and just as well because I was stopped at Customs. I was very nervous. I guess anyone would be. I told the Customs official why I was bringing so many toys home for Christmas but for some reason or another they didn't believe me. They kept me at the airport for two hours and even took a copy of my passport. At that stage I felt they were treating me like a criminal and I just told them to keep everything. I eventually told them to call my ma and she told them the whole story. Thank God, they believed her and allowed me to keep everything. I think they thought that I had stolen the toys and was bringing them home to sell.

In the end though, the hassle at Customs was well worthwhile. It made those poor kids so happy on Christmas morning. I remember my ma would leave letters from Betty to the kids at Christmas telling them how good they were for Martha (my ma) and to continue to be good and that she would always be watching them. On a sunny day when we would all be sitting in the kitchen and the sun would shine through the back door my ma would say to the kids, *"Look, there's Betty smiling down at you. She's very happy because you are all very good."* And then at night-time she would lie in bed with them and look out at the stars and say to the kids, *"The biggest star is God, the second biggest is Our Lady and the third biggest is your mammy. She is letting you know that she can see you but you can't see her."*

Those kids cried for the longest time, day after day, night after night and my ma cried with them. My ma also had to deal with tantrums the kids had for a long time. I swear it wasn't easy. The morning of Betty's death her kids were all staying in different houses and each and every one of them swore that they had seen their mother. Betty appeared to them all at the bottom of their beds. They were actually able to describe which way she was sitting on the bed before them. It is a bit scary but little kids wouldn't make something like that up so I believe it.

The whole situation was very hard for my ma and da at the beginning, especially financially as they were only getting forty pounds a week for all the kids. This was very little money to support five kids but being my ma somehow she managed; I guess she had no choice. The eldest of the five kids, Leonda lived with my granny while Nicola, Carly, Roslyn and Alan stayed with my ma and Da. All the girls went to St Mary's School in Baldoyle and have done very well for themselves while Alan, the youngest, is still at school. I think these kids are a credit to my ma and da. And I know Betty would be just so happy with how they turned out.

However, sadly, I don't think to this day that any of Betty's friends are alive. They all died as a result of drug abuse. One lad from the inner city was so affected by all of the young dying that he wrote a song which was often played at their funerals. Called '*A wasted life at seventeen*' the song tells of a young boy leaving school at seventeen with no work and no dole and he asks his dad the question '*Is this going to be my role?*' *Hanging around the cafés all day, the pushers find the boy easy prey and ask him to try a fix. They told him it would make him feel good.* The words of that song were poignant as they told so much of the truth about what was going on

A lot of young people started off by looking for just one fix and this led them down the one-way road to death. As the numbers of young people losing their lives to drugs in the inner city rose, a monument was erected by the community. It was moulded together using pieces of gold from the jewellery belonging to the young people who died. It is located in Killarney Street outside St. Joseph's Mansions and every year a Mass is said and a commemoration held at the monument to remember the dead. This means a lot to their families

Betty's best friend's life was also shattered by drugs. I want to tell her story because she was so close to Betty, and her ma is a fine example of how hard families fought to save their loved ones and it shows too how hard the poor addicts fought to have better lives, even though there was no help available. Lizo Reilly was from Sheriff Street and Betty and Lizo became friends through Maureen, Lizo's sister, and Jenny, Betty's sister. Whenever Maureen and Jenny went to see each other they always took their younger sisters along with them and this is how their friendship started. Like Betty, Lizo was only seventeen when she first smoked hash. Once she got a taste for drugs she moved onto tablets which then led to her using needles. Lizo became heavily dependent on drugs and like Betty she robbed to feed her habit. She was caught, of course, and spent a few years in and out of prison. As Lizo was part of a big family and the only one to go on drugs her mother didn't know what the hell was happening to her daughter. She knew she was changing and that something was happening to her as her speech became slower and she was always restless. Her whole personality changed as well. When her mother found out that she was on drugs, she was devastated. She tried to get help for her but at that time there was no help for addicts in the inner city. After a few years the drug problem had moved out to the suburbs of Dublin. Once the middle-class areas started to be affected by drugs, everyone started to sit up and pay attention and suddenly the drug problem became one that had to be dealt with. Lizo's mother went to seek help in the Rutland Centre but it was for private patients only and Lizo's treatment would have cost three thousand five hundred pounds. Now where in the name of God was this woman going to get that kind of money? So unfortunately Lizo had to suffer on with no help. She just had to try to kick the habit on her own and, of course, with the help of her family. But little did she know what a hold it had taken on her life. She could not fight it on her own, not even with the help of her family. She needed serious help, professional help. Once the government started to address the problem, drug treatment clinics were set up around the inner city and this is where Lizo went to seek help as did Betty. Lizo was put on a methadone programme. Methadone is also a drug but it is prescribed by a doctor and the amount is also controlled by a doctor at the centre. It helps addicts to come down off hard drugs and also to stop risking their lives sharing dirty needles. A urine sample has to be produced each day to show the clinic that other drugs are not being abused. But you know what annoys me is that while they were trying to get off drugs and stay on the methadone programme, there were pushers selling them sleeping tablets telling them that they would help them to sleep. How in the name of God was there any hope for these people?

Lizo was doing great for a while and eventually met and fell in love with the father of her two children, but he was on drugs too. Now Lizo loved this man very much and would have done anything for him. Both he and her children were her life. She was a wonderful mother and was starting to get back on her feet now that she was off heroin. She even decided to do a back-to-school course where she met someone very special, Mother Teresa. Lizo was very religious and always wore a miraculous medal around her neck. So when Lizo saw Mother Teresa she was the happiest girl in the world and made it her business to have a special chat with her.

Their chat was private and from that day to this no one knows what that conversation was about. But Lizo made sure she got her photo taken with her and she was the only one who did. She was overjoyed and it gave her a lot of hope in life. To meet Mother Teresa was a blessing from God to Lizo. However, one day Lizo got word that her boyfriend and soul mate had died of a drug overdose. This nearly killed her and she went back on drugs heavily. Only this time she also felt she really wanted to be with him and life could not go on without him. As she walked down by the River Liffey outside the Custom House one day, Lizo tried to commit suicide. Luckily there was a man hanging around the quayside drinking and he jumped into the Liffey after her and saved her life. She was brought to the Mater Hospital but released the next day without any help or counselling being offered. Lizo tried very hard to get on with her life and moved back in with her mother. This was where she felt safe, where she had someone special to watch and love her every minute of the day. The flats had been knocked down by this time and Lizo's ma had a lovely house in Sheriff Street and she kept rabbits in her garden. Lizo was out playing with the rabbits in the back garden one nice quiet afternoon while her ma was in the kitchen looking out the window peeling the potatoes. She heard an ambulance going by and she just blessed herself and said, *"God help them whoever they are."*

Just shortly after that there was a knock on the door and it was the police to tell Mrs. Reilly that her daughter Lizo had thrown herself underneath a train at Amiens Street Station. Her mother nearly dropped dead herself with the shock to her system. Once again Lizo survived this second suicide attempt but it left her in a wheelchair as she lost one of her legs. The whole of Sheriff Street was devastated as she was loved by everybody. She again tried to get her life together and this time she lived in a flat on her own even though she was in a wheelchair. There was still no stopping her. She had the fight in her once again and would not give up and she still had the sense of humour to go with it. All the kids in Sheriff Street loved her and they would wheel her around everywhere in the wheel chair and every week when she had to go to the post office to collect her money one of the kids would always take her. You would hear her shouting in Sheriff Street whether it was across the street to someone or up the road. There was always a 'how a ya' on the go. Even though she was left in a wheelchair she still went around with a smile. A few years later she got an electric wheel-chair with a basket in front so she could get her few messages and, of course, her few cans of Tennants. Then this made the smile brighter. She loved her few cans of Tennants, whenever she had the money to buy them. There was one other thing that Lizo loved and that was cabbage water and, Jesus, if that cabbage water was given to someone else Lizo cursed them from a height and called them all the names under the sun. So her mother made sure she got it every Sunday. Lizo eventually lost both her parents and this was so hard for her to deal with. But despite all the bad things that life brought her it also brought her a lot of good things, especially the strength to carry on in life. Lizo died in 2003 leaving her loving kids, family and friends behind and Sheriff Street will never be the same without her. But I believe she is in heaven today with the people she loved so much, her parents, boyfriend, best friend Betty and Mother Teresa. Her funeral was very sad but the crowd was huge and you couldn't get into the church. One of the gifts brought up at the offertory was her wheelchair.

My uncle Tommy was next to go. Tommy was a painter but he had an accident and won a big insurance claim. He received twenty-seven thousand pounds for a back injury, and 25 years ago that was a lot of money. He spent most of the money in the pubs with his friends; in fact he drank until it was gone. He shared some of his money with his family and he took good care of his partner, Maeve. She had two kids with him and four kids from a previous marriage. He died of liver disease because of his drinking. Tommy could be funny at times, and was forever telling jokes. I remember he would say to me every time I met him, *"You know, Jenna, I'm your uncle, right?"*

"Yeah, Tommy."

"Well, does that mean it's OK for me to ask your boyfriend Paul's ma for a loan of a fiver?"

This made me laugh. Paul's ma lived above Tommy at this stage. He always gave the fiver back on a Friday and then borrowed it again the following Monday. Ah, he was a good man but like many of them he just went the wrong direction.

The last one to die in my ma's family was Bimbo. Bimbo was my ma's brother but his real name was Francis. He was another victim of drugs. I liked Bimbo a lot and I know he really liked me. He was good-natured and kind but drugs just took over his life. He died of a drug overdose. Before Bimbo ever went on drugs he had everything in life that he wanted. He lived in Bayside with his beautiful wife, Margaret, and their son, Gary. He had a taxi which at that time going back about twenty-five years was a big thing and he also had a caravan shop outside Bayside train station. He had a good life until one day it all fell apart. His marriage ended, his house was sold and his wife and son went to live in England. Unfortunately Bimbo couldn't deal with this and fell into a depression that week by week got deeper and deeper. With only one person to turn to, his friend said to him, *"Here try this fix; it will make you feel much better."*

Of course, with wanting to get better he thought he was doing the right thing but didn't know that this was going to lead to the end. Soon he found himself with nothing. Bimbo would often say to people, *"Look, I have one house in this arm and another house in that."* What he meant, of course, was that he was injecting drugs into his arms and all the money that he had wasted on drugs could have been spent on a nice house and a happier family life, instead of heroin. But not realising the consequences, there was no turning back for Bimbo; well, at least, not back then. Now there are treatment centres and drop-in clinics; addicts are given their own needles instead of sharing needles like they did a long time ago. There is counselling and I guess it's more open these days with information being given to kids at a young age in school. There is a greater awareness of the dangers of drugs but still hundreds of young people make what they see as a lifestyle choice to get involved in taking drugs. They call them recreational drugs but if they could see the consequences down the road they might think differently.

But good people around the city tried to stop the young kids getting into trouble or involved in taking drugs. My uncle, for example, started a boxing club in town to help keep young people off the streets and out of trouble. Such people were looked up to by young kids so they were more inclined to join the club. The community workers tried very hard to help young people and to show them what being a criminal can do to your life and that there was another, better way to live that did not involve crime and death. But back in the time of Mary, Betty and Bimbo the outlook for young people in the inner city was very bleak. And they were from just one family, our family. But this was happening in every family in the inner city. It was a sad five years for my ma's family and I just don't know how my granny got through it at all. She must have been a very strong woman but to this day she still cries over the loss of her children. Drink and drugs certainly took a very heavy toll on our family.

6

Throughout all of the hard times my ma made a very happy home life for all of us in St Joseph's Mansions and I have thousands of great memories of my childhood in Joey's.

When I was four years old I started school in Rutland Street off Summerhill, not too far from where we lived. Children from all the surrounding flats went to school here. We didn't have to wear a uniform back then and we went swimming with the school to Sean MacDermott Street Baths and put on musicals. Mrs Cunningham was the head teacher in Rutland Street when we started and I remember her as being very kind. Rutland Street School was where Anita and I started our lifelong friendship. The teachers made us very welcome. They were very dedicated to helping us to learn and be interested in education. This wasn't easy because of where we were living. My family was a happy one but not every child in that school had it easy at home.

When I went into the classroom that first day I met my

second cousin and best friend, Anita Burke, for the first time in my life. Anita had been living in Birmingham but moved back to Ireland with her parents in 1972. Anita and I made our First Holy Communion together in Matt Talbot Church in Lower Sean MacDermott Street, when we were just seven. It was a great day. Getting dressed up for First Holy Communion with all the trimmings was very important in the inner city and I felt very special. No expense was spared on that day. After the church we went around to all of our cousins to collect a few bob and, of course, for us kids this was the best bit even though I felt like a princess in the church. But then off we went around visiting the family. In every house all you heard the women saying was, *"Ah look at her! Jaysus, isn't she the image of her Aunt Betty?"*

"Jaysus, no, I think she is the image of Jenny."

That would be on the mother's side of the family. Then you would visit the da's side of the family and you would hear it all over again,

"Jaysus, she's the image of Annie's daughter."

Well, that would go on all day. I would just say to myself, 'Well I am the image of myself'. I swear in every house that you would go to there would be a cup of tea and about ten cigarettes for my ma. Your communion outfit would be stinking of smoke by the end of the day and yet they would be afraid to give you something to eat in case you got it dirty.

My cousin Anita was just the funniest and always made me laugh. In fact, she still does. She would call for me on the way to school every morning and, standing at the bottom of the stairs up to our flat she would shout up,

"Jenna, Jenna, Jenna bleeding Cahill, I'm going to school."

I'd have to hurry up but I would be laughing at her because Anita always took going to school very seriously. Anita and I used to hold hands going to school every morning. Most mornings we would run up to the twenty-seven steps at Summerhill to meet our teacher so that we could tell her where we were in our books. We always tried to do better than everyone else when it came to our school work even though we were only in second class at this stage. Anita was very smart at school and she could have been anything she wanted if she had had the opportunity. As for me, I was also smart and I knew how important education was if you wanted to get ahead in life.

In third class we moved up to what was called 'big school' and this is when we came across a very cross teacher who had our lives scalded. Oh, my God, this man was tough. He was always out with the stick if you were late to school or even just made a mistake saying your prayers. Whatever the reason, he was always out with the stick, waving it around the place, ready to plant it on somebody. I used to feel sorry for the young fellas as they used to get killed for basically doing nothing. I used to say to myself, 'One day this man is going to do some serious damage.' Anita and I were late one day for school and we were scared because we knew we were going to be killed so we made a plan.

"Anita, I'm not going to allow him to hit me," I said.
"Neither am I, Jenna," replied Anita.

So off we went into school and, of course, he wanted to hit us for being late. So straightaway we refused to put our hands out to be slapped. We were thrown out of school for just that. But, you know, I really didn't care because I knew we were right. But we didn't tell our parents because we would have been killed by them as well. I don't know where we planned to go each morning but we were not going to school. A few days later we were outside the school gate wondering how we were going to get back in when we saw himself going towards his car. We ran over to his car.

"We're sorry. Can we come back to school?"

"Yes," he said, hopping into the car. I remember he took us to the shop and bought us a chocolate 'Catch' bar. We were both so happy to be back in school that day because if our mas had found out they would have killed us altogether. I have to admit though that I was thrown out of school a few more times after that for one reason or another. But to tell you the truth that teacher just got mad at you for no reason at all. Another teacher, Mr. M., was very nice most of the time but, Jesus, when he got mad he would get the duster and throw it at you and the saliva would be running down from his mouth with annoyance. Sometimes you couldn't blame the teachers for getting mad because the classes were huge and it made it hard to give every child the attention they needed. Most of the kids were interested in learning but, of course, you always got the dossers. A great aspect of school was that our mothers didn't have to make lunch for us to take to school. We got fresh sandwiches every day and raisin buns on Wednesdays. Sometimes we brought lunch though

because we thought that they used margarine on the bread. And you would never dare eat margarine in our house. That was not on at all. You would be the talk of the flats if your mother used margarine. Rutland Street was a great school but I think we all would have enjoyed it more and learnt more if we hadn't been half killed almost every day. Looking back I know that most of the young fellas in my class ended up in trouble with the police or on drugs. When I watched them growing up around me, I knew in my heart that you really had to be a very strong kid to survive growing up in the flats.

I spent a lot of time in Anita's flat. Anita's ma and da were lovely people and they were a very close family. I was always welcome in their flat but sometimes we drove Skinner, Anita's da, mad. Eventually he would say to us, *"Will you's go out and play with the heavy traffic?"*

And you know what? We did. Back then you could hop on and off the old buses because they were open at the back. When they came around by Joseph's Mansions, we would hop on and then down the road we would hop off again. Now when I think back to it that was a dangerous game to be playing but at that age we thought it was great fun altogether. But Skinner was just the best. I remember when white pump runners were all the rage in town and the whiter they were the better. Skinner would paint Anita's and, I tell you, they were the whitest pumps you could get and the envy of everyone. I laughed at Skinner when he did this. Skinner was also famous for his porridge and when he had a pot made in the morning he would shout over the balcony into our flat,

"Martha, Martha, does Jenna want to come over for a bit of porridge?"

They knew I loved porridge so they were very happy to see me eat it. I had been very sick as a baby and had spent a long time in hospital. I suppose they all worried about me and were delighted to see me eat.

But when he had a few drinks on him, Skinner would call me and, I don't know why, but, he always spilled his heart out to me. And he still does that. I had a visit with Skinner recently and every time I go in he makes me laugh from the time I go in to him to the time I leave. This time he said to me, *"Jenna, you're lucky you rang the door bell or you wouldn't have gotten in."*

"Why is that, Skinner?" says I.

"Ah, Jen, it's only new and I want everyone to keep it ringing."

To this day Skinner still lives in town, in the Gloucester Diamond and nearly all of his children come to visit him every day. He is always in his bedroom. I tell you he never leaves that bedroom and if anything ever happens to him, we'll have to bury him there. He told me a while ago when I was in with him, *"Jen I went up town a few weeks ago you know, up to the confession box"*.

I said, *"What, Skinner, did you go up to tell all your sins?"* I was being serious, and he started to laugh. *"Not the bleeding confession box, the pub."*

Now how did I not cop on to that one? I think I'm out of the inner city too long. I think he must be one of the last great old Dublin characters. One of his sons comes every Wednesday and Saturday and brings Skinner his Lotto. The girls come in every day and clean his house and Tracey, the eldest daughter, is always cleaning the windows. I have to say they are good to him and he will never be lonely. But he still thinks he has to feed the nation. When I go in, no matter what time of the day, I am offered some dinner. He keeps a big pot of stew on the cooker every day.

"Skinner," I always ask him, *"who is all that dinner for?"*

"Jen," he always replies, *"anyone that comes in here, there's a bit of dinner for them. Sure I send over to the neighbours and ask them do they want some too."*

"Skinner, you're gas"

When I was leaving that day he handed me an orange and a banana for my son Jonathan and said, *"Jen, tell him fruit is good for his teeth."*

He gets that from his late wife Mary, Anita's ma. Mary always made sure we ate well. To this day I remember that she always had loads of fruit in her house and she made sure we ate plenty of it. And that was before we even knew it was good for you. But much of the food that we ate when we were kids was very different to the food the kids eat today. Back then parents gave their kids loads of sugar on bread and they would even dip the babies' soothers in sugar and put it in their mouths to keep them quiet. No wonder the kids had problems with their teeth growing up. One treat I loved was 'guddie'. Oh, God, I have to say it was gorgeous. A few slices of bread were broken up into little bite-size pieces and put into a cup. Then a little butter and sugar were added and finally boiling water. When it was all mashed up together it tasted gorgeous and was warm and filling on a winter's day.

During the week meals were always eaten in a hurry but I'll never forget the Sunday dinners we had. Sunday was a special day and the smell of the corned beef and cabbage that would meet you when you walked up the stairs to the flat after Sunday Mass was amazing. My ma always got loads of meat in for Sunday dinner and you could have your choice. We had chicken and roast beef or corned beef and tons of vegetables and, of course, spuds. While the dinner was cooking my da played records of all the famous ballets and he would have it so loud you could hear music all over the flats. And, of course, dessert was always jelly and ice cream, bought fresh on the way home from Mass. I loved those Sundays. They felt extra special, I feel, because you ate food that you would not have any other day of the week so it tasted nicer. We had no freezer so ice cream was only bought for a treat. In town we all did our shopping in local shops and in the markets and the traders knew all the regulars that came into their shops and knew all about each family. Going to the shops was like going to confession for some people as they aired all their ailments and problems to whoever would listen. There was always someone to talk to about your problems in those days and you wouldn't need therapy as long as there were people to listen to you and where we lived there were always willing ears. Mr. Dooley had his shop just around the corner from us and it was very popular with us kids because he stocked a lot of fancy goods and sweets and stationery and bits and bobs. This is where Anita and I went to buy each other a present for our birthdays. I would buy her a box of Maltesers and a week later when it was my birthday she would buy me a box.

We did this for years. Another favourite haunt of ours was Mary's Chipper up in Summer Hill. Mary, the owner, was a friend of a Mrs. Redmond who lived underneath us at St Joseph's Mansions. So, my ma being very smart, and us being very hungry, every time we were sent to the chipper she would say, *"Tell Mary they're for Mrs. Redmond and she will give you loads"*

So off we would go up to the chipper and right enough Mary would pile the steaming chunky chips up into the little white greaseproof bags until we thought they were going to topple over. Then she would grab them up into the newspaper, wrapping them tightly the way they wouldn't escape on our return journey. I have to say she was very generous and knew my ma had a load of mouths to feed. My ma would send us for fifty pence or a pound's worth but what we came back with must have been worth at least five times that. Across the street from St Joseph's was the nicest fruit and vegetable shop and every summer whenever I had money I would go over and buy gooseberries and plums. Oh, they were just gorgeous, freshly bought each morning from the fruit market. When I went over to the shop I was always asking the owner questions as I was always fascinated and curious about shops and how they worked as a business. I was thinking ahead. Now I'll never forget this particular shop because it had a gumball machine in the window. It cost two pounds fifty and I really wanted it for my birthday one year but back then two pounds fifty was a lot of money. My ma and da said they wouldn't buy it for me but I cried and cried and, of course, I got my own way and they ended up buying it for me. I was very happy then once I had got my own way. I know now as a parent that it is very hard to say no to your children when they have their hearts set on something.

Beside the shop was the presbytery where the priest lived. As kids we went over there to visit a good few times and we were always made welcome. We would be brought into the cosy sitting-room and sometimes we would get tea and biscuits and we would just sit around and have a chat. This was great for us kids especially on rainy nights when we had nowhere else to go. I don't know what we talked about but I suppose we gave our opinion on everything and the priest was always glad to hear it.

Religion was very important in town and the priests were very good to the people in their community. Everyone went to Mass and this was a must in our family too. All the old people, of course, went because they were always worried about their souls but the reason I liked it was that they always had a Children's Mass, with lots of singing. My favourite song was 'Jesus is the rock' because there were actions to go with it and I always loved singing and dancing. We were young and carefree and we didn't question anything but their faith was very important to the families that were losing people to drugs. It helped them to endure the hard times and they were comforted by their religion as they tried to understand why their son or daughter or brother or sister had died so young. It was all that got them through because they had little else to hold onto. But, as for now, I can honestly say I don't know how long it is since I went to Mass but I know that it's years. *"Isn't that terrible?"*

Almost as important as Mass was the nightly pilgrimage to Bingo. Anita's ma, Mary, went to the Macushla Hall every night for her regular ration of bingo. Loads of women from the flats used to go. Oh, my God, but Mary's bingo was very important to her. She would never ever miss a night. And she had a nightly routine as well that she thought brought her luck. In St Joseph's there were always rats in the pram shed, so Mary, on her way out to bingo, would stop at the pram shed and have a few words with the rats. Anita and I would be looking over the balcony laughing our heads off at her. Ah, but Mary and Skinner were the greatest and I loved them.

Down in the yard of the flats, we had ropes tied around the washing line poles and about five of us would be swinging out of one pole at the same time. It was gas; the more there were on the swings the better fun it was. We would just keep going around for hours and hours. Sometimes you would have the mothers giving out because; their washing would fall off the lines. They would go mad especially if they had to wash it again. Ah, there was always someone giving out. But overall they were okay. And many a night the women would come out and sit on the steps and have a chat with us. They were really good times. We would be out all day playing and our parents never saw us from morning to night except when we got hungry.

I didn't like when my da used to call us up for bed at nine o'clock every night. You would hear him shouting,

"Jenna, Miriam, James, come on up for bed."

"Ah, da, give us five more minutes."

No matter what we were doing we always seemed to need five more minutes. At the weekends he allowed us to stay out a little bit later and on Friday night when my da got paid he would bring home big Jaffa oranges, Granny Smith apples and a large bar of Dairy Milk chocolate. Oh and he never forgot his bar of Fry's Cream for himself. Yea Friday night was very special.

Saturday was special too. My ma would make a beautiful salad for dinner and then she would send us kids around to Talbot Street to get apple and jam cakes from the Bakery. They were gorgeous. I tell you when my ma would call us up for dinner on a Saturday we always ran up because her food was so great. And sometimes rather than buying the cakes, she would bake apple cakes with us. We didn't have a rolling pin so we used a glass milk bottle to roll out the pastry. I loved when she baked with us. My happiest memories are of the things we did together as a family. These did not have to be big outings or trips but the small little traditions that made me feel so secure and loved. Do you remember when *Dallas* was the big television show that everyone watched and raved about? It was on RTÉ on a Tuesday night and I just loved this night because all of our family used to sit around and watch the programme together. I especially loved it because my ma always put her legs up on my da's lap and then I knew that they loved each other. It was a good feeling for me and I went to bed happy in the knowledge that they were in love. To this day I have never told my ma or da that.

7

The summers in the flats were the best. And my most constant memory of sunny days is of my Aunt Mary. Like a waitress in a hotel she would bring down tea for all the ladies on a silver tray down into the yard of the flats. As she was bringing it down the steps she would shout out the same words each time, *"You wouldn't get this in the Gresham Hotel."* She made a great occasion out of bringing down that tea and it always made us laugh. On really hot days our mothers sunbathed in their bras and, Jesus, some of the women would use cooking oil to get a tan. I always thought as a kid that they were mad but you know if you laughed at them sitting there cooking themselves and sipping tea they would roar at you, *"Children should be seen and not heard."* That was their motto so it was best to say nothing. On the really hot summer days everybody, young and old from all four blocks, would sit out. There were four benches, one for each block and late into the night during the summer months the women would sit down on the benches and have their chats and their cups of tea. As long as the women were out, we kids would stay out playing. And while we were playing we would have great singsongs. The songs could be heard around all four blocks we were so loud. When it got later into the night some parent, usually a mother, would come out and shout over the balcony, *"Will you ever shut up, you pack of crows? The kids are trying to sleep."* There was never any harm in their words. They would only be messing when they called us crows. Anyone that came through the gates those late summer evenings would come over to whoever was out on the benches and stop and have a chat and a cup of tea before going up to bed. No one was lonely in the flats. There would always be someone looking out for you and there for you if you were in trouble.

Around A and B blocks it was mostly all of us cousins who set out our blankets on the ground against the pram shed and, stripped to our bikinis, we would sit out from morning until night, only going home for something to eat when we were starving. When we got bored we danced. We were always dancing as kids and on sunny days in the flats when we wanted to practise we would bring the record player outside to the front of the pram shed. The needle of the old player usually needed a little help to stay on the record so we would have to use a ten-pence piece to hold the needle down. We knew every trick of the trade. I remember one particular day we were all outside dancing to a song called 'Everybody salsa, everybody salsa'. We started off dancing in one long line facing out from the shed to the front gate of the flats. The people passing by in their cars were taking a quick glance in when they heard the sound of the music and our yelps and screams of delight and happiness. One by one even the girls that were shy joined in and soon enough the line of dancers stretched out to the front gate of the playground. It was magic that day. The sun was splitting the trees; the women were sitting on the steps of the flats watching while others leant over their balconies. As we got a little older and wanted to have our own space and feel a bit more grown up and independent we pooled some money between the whole lot of us and I decided that we should go down to the Wimpy café in Parnell Street. I asked the owner if we could block a part off especially for ourselves as we would like to have a party. There was no problem with this as we were bringing custom to his café. We paid for chips and burgers for the whole gang of us. He wouldn't allow us to bring down our own record player though and this was hard because a party is not a party without music. But he had a juke box that we could use. So out of the left-over money we fed his juke box with money all night. The café was empty that night apart from our gang. It never did any business though, so soon after that it closed down and that was the end of our wild parties.

When we weren't in the playground in the evening time, and not playing our other games and maybe just wanting some time on our own, we always had our skates. The old skates had four wheels, two in the front and two at the back, and were kept on with a buckle. The buckle would eventually rust and fall off and we would have to use our ma's nylon tights to wrap around them to keep them on our feet. Sometimes we would be killed because we might have made off with our ma's good and maybe last pair of tights. But we usually played together as a big gang and planned our adventures for the day. One hot summer's evening time when the playground was closed, we were all together down in the flats thinking of what we didn't have. The inner city on a hot summer's day was sweltering with no gentle sea breeze to cool us down. We decided that day that we wanted a swimming pool in the flats as it was the one thing we hadn't got. The more we thought about it the more we got our brains working and decided that, yes, we could do it. We all went home and got every shovel and spade we could get our hands on and threw them over the railings of the playground to empty the sand out of the sandpit. The sandpit would be our swimming pool. Now this was not a small sandpit. It would have been big enough but, of course, not deep enough for a swimming pool. We did a good job, we thought, between us and went to bed happy that night, thinking what a great day we were going to have in our swimming pool the following day. As the next sunny day dawned we all headed down to the playground with our bikinis on. Lady Reilly, the woman in charge of the playground, was waiting for us and we could see by her face that she was not very impressed at all. This wasn't going to happen as far as she was concerned because there was no way she was going to be responsible. All the sand had to be put back in. Soon after that our dream of a swimming pool was completely shattered as the sandpit was filled with cement. I guess part of the reason for this was that our mothers were probably sick and tired of all the nits we got in our hair from the sand.

*　*　*

My ma took us kids to Dollymount beach during the summer when we were on our summer holidays from school. It was a tradition in the inner city and on a sunny morning the queues for the Number 30 or 44A buses would snake down the street as families made their way to the bus stop laden down with spades and water rings, rugs and prams, footballs and baskets of food for the day. All of us five kids went and most of the time Anita and her sister Margaret came with us for company. We never went to the main beach because my ma found her own little spot one year and from that day on she always called it her 'private beach' and of course we believed her. She always brought a big picnic because you would be gone for the day if it was really sunny and there were no shops near the beach. So, everything had to be brought in that picnic basket to keep our gang from starving and complaining. There would be piles of sandwiches with every filling, bottles of lemonade, tons of packets of biscuits and, of course, you could not go without the big flask of tea and the milk on the side. I have to say my ma would not have enjoyed the beach without her cup of tea and she really loved the beach. We would leave the flats about eleven o'clock in the morning when the weather had decided what it was going to do for the day and we would stay on the beach until my ma had to go to work that evening. We would stay until the very latest minute but we knew she needed time to give us our dinner before she left for work every day. And, of course, being very house-proud the place had to be shining before she left for work because she hated coming back to a dirty home.

Sometimes for a change we went to the beach at Portmarnock. I loved going there because there was a stall that sold buckets, spades and what have you and I remember Miriam and I would ask the man could we help and he always allowed us to. That was my favourite beach of the two because of this.

And talking of the beach reminds me that nearly everyone in the flats collected winkles. They were everywhere, and every day there would be someone selling them down in the flats. You could get about three winkles for a penny. And, boy, they were gorgeous. Sometime you would get the odd kid selling the winkles that were already eaten. They would be messing, of course, and chancing their arms but you know kids; any opportunity to be little devils. Winkles were sold wrapped in newspaper. We used to go out to Howth to collect ours. When we were out there on the summer project, we would collect them and take them home in the evening.

*   *   *

In town we were one of the few flats that had a playground with a shed and playleaders. The playleaders were the ladies that took care of us kids when we were down in the yard. It was a great idea because our mothers couldn't keep an eye on us all day. It is not like living in a house where you can just look out your window every minute to watch your child playing in the garden. Our mothers had to try to keep an eye on us and do their work and that was not easy when you were four floors up in your flat.

The 'ladies' as we called them were hired by Dublin Corporation. The only playground close by that had play-leaders was Hill Street just off Parnell Street. And sometimes the playleaders would organise competitions between the two playgrounds. God, we practised so hard for these competitions in both sports and dancing and singing. The corporation sponsored these events and the winning playground received a trophy as their prize. I was very competitive as a child and, boy, did I want to win and if I didn't I would go into a sulk. I would be happy for the winners but I would have been even happier if we had won. But we did win a lot of the time. We had a lot of talent in our playground and the playleaders worked so hard to encourage us and make us into real stars. No expense was spared and our costumes were magnificent. When we put on a show we went all out and gave it everything.

* * *

Now it wasn't always about cups of tea. Sometimes you would hear one of the neighbours having a fight and you knew the father would have come in drunk. I remember as a kid looking out my bedroom window each night to see if I could see what was going on. It was better than television and then the next day everyone would be gossiping about what had happened the night before. The only time I really got nervous was when my da came in drunk. I know my ma and da had their rows but I don't remember hearing their fights. Well, maybe I didn't want to hear. But it could be funny. When my Uncle Skinner would come in drunk, my cousin Margaret would run over to our house, crying. So we would take care of her. It was a well-known fact that Margaret and I were the cowards of the family because we always got scared when our das came in drunk. There would be many a night when my da would come in the gate of the flats shouting, *"Up the Dubs!"*

Then Skinner, Anita's da, would come in the other gate shouting, *"Ireland is my country."*

I don't know what they thought they were shouting about but I don't suppose they cared either. They were well full of drink. Back then nearly all the das spent the evenings in the pubs and sometimes it was funny to look at them making eejits of themselves.

* * *

Every summer there was a 'summer project' organised by the corporation in the inner city. It was like a summer camp I suppose and all of the kids were brought on day trips as part of it. The summer projects were brilliant because they kept the kids off the streets. There was always something going on or being organised so you would never be bored. And if the weather was too hot a water fight would start up and all the kids from the different blocks would join in. And, of course, summer projects and clowning around outdoors always brought a few trips to Temple Street Hospital for one or other of us. One day when I was heading back home after playing in the sand-pit I was knocked over by a bike. I had a metal spade in my hand and it just ripped my leg open. Diane was with me and she went running home to my ma crying her eyes out. I wasn't crying but when I got to Temple St Hospital, oh my God, I swear that's when I started to cry. I got twenty-five stitches that day and I will never forget it. I cried my eyes out. God help my poor ma because there was always one of us in Casualty for one reason or another. And sometimes there could be two of us waiting to be either stitched or X-rayed. It was like a second home to us in the inner city and we would have been lost without it. To this day my ma still has the same problems but I guess that's what happens when you have a lot of kids. Well, I got thirty-five stitches at different stages in my life, and I was just one kid.

In the playground there was a hut big enough to hold all of us kids. It came in handy on rainy days as we could take shelter and run out again when the rain stopped. It was also a place for all of the kids to come together and sit and chat and have a laugh.

The games were constant and fantastic. We played skipping and sometimes even the women would join in our games. As kids we thought this was great fun altogether. There were two women in the flats who were sisters and they never married or had kids of their own, but they were very good to all the other kids especially the little ones. Anyway these two ladies were forever playing with the kids. Even if we played 'Piggy' the women would join in. 'Piggy' was great fun. Eight boxes were placed on the ground which was marked out with chalk into boxes with the numbers one to eight inside. To start off your go you threw a can of polish into a box and you had to hop through the eight boxes without putting a foot into the box with the can. If the box landed on a line you were out and the next person got a go. Whoever reached the eighth box first won the game but sometimes we played it backwards just so the game would last longer. Skipping was one of my favourite games because everyone could join in even the adults including the two spinster sisters. The other reason I liked it was because we used to sing songs while we skipped and as I have told you already I was always singing and dancing. One of the songs we sang was . . .

> "VOTE, VOTE, VOTE FOR DE VALERA.
> IN WALKS MIRIAM AT THE DOOR.
> MIRIAM IS THE ONE THAT WILL HAVE A BIT
> OF FUN
> AND WE DON'T WANT JENNA ANY MORE."

Everyone would stand in a line and skip through the rope one after the other. There would be gangs of us in this line; the more the merrier. Now the boys never played these games because if they even attempted to they would be called cissies and that was not cool at all. 'Two balls against the wall' was another popular game. One of the songs that went with this game was 'Billie bowler, biscuit baker, Ballybough and Ballsbridge', not easy to say and keep a ball in the air at the same time. The game was over when the ball fell and you had to start all over again. We also played 'kiss chasing' where the boys chased the girls and when you were caught the boy had to kiss you. The games were just never-ending.

Sunday afternoon was a day for all the friends to do something together. Myself and all the girls from the flats would get together and do something most Sundays. If there was a good film on at the pictures we would go down to the Savoy and try to bunk in. Sometimes we got caught, but most of the time we bunked in, no problem. This was best because then we had more money to spend on sweets, or maybe go to Burger King on the way home. If we went to see a musical we would wait for the singing part to come on and then we would all join in clapping our hands in the air and singing along with the movie. After the film we would go back to the flats and try to act out the whole movie ourselves. Other Sundays we would go to the airport to the café and get something to eat and then go into the bathrooms. We were always fascinated by the bathrooms; I suppose because our bathrooms at home were pretty basic. When we went into the bathrooms we would put money into the sanitary towel machines and some of the girls would put them on just to see what it was like. If we weren't off to the movies or the airport we would all head up to the Zoo. Off we would go up on the number ten bus and, yes, we would sometimes go around to see the animals but I swear we rarely made it past the café. We spent most of the time just sitting, eating and chatting away. As teenagers we loved going into cafés. I suppose it made us feel very grown-up, like our parents. We tried to bunk into the Zoo as well so that we could keep our money for the café, but if we thought it was going to be too hard we knew that it wasn't even worth the try. We always stuck together as cousins and friends and loved each other and looked out for one another. But we could be pretty terrible to one another as well. One day one of us got her period but, of course, we were afraid to go to the shop for tampons. So we sent my Aunt Jenny's young fella for them. He was only about seven at that time. We just wrote a note for him and behind it all, of course, we were laughing our hearts out. In fairness to him he did come back with them.

The one funny and loving thing that I really liked about living in the flats was when you would hear voices from all four blocks at different times. My ma might shout *"Miriam, will you run up to your granny and ask her for a bit of butter?"*

Then you would hear someone else shouting, *"Are you coming up for a cup of tea?"*

"I'll be up in a minute," would be the reply.

Then some kid would shout up, *"Are you coming out to play?"*

Well, that was the only way to communicate in those days in the flats because no one had a telephone and if you had you were the talk of the flats and everyone thought you were rich. We had to use our imagination when it came to playing games and we were never short of ideas. I remember I got a plastic Wendy Playhouse for a present one time. I really loved that Wendy House. As a kid I wanted to have a shop so I thought to myself one day you know I could start a shop right here. And I did. Even as a small child I was already thinking of ways to make money because I hated asking my ma and da for money. Anyway I don't know where I got the money from but I got it from somewhere and I headed to the local shop. The first thing I bought was a packet of Kimberley biscuits. That's grand, I thought to myself. I'll make a few pence profit on this packet if I open it and sell the biscuits separately. I knew that making a profit was very important. At the end of each day I would count my money and see how much of a profit I had made for that hard day's work. I had my own little song too that I used to sing during shop hours. It went like this,

"Buy away, buy away, new shop open, ham, jam anything you want, ma'am."

It always felt good to have something of my own and I hoped that one day I might own a big shop. I had a lot of other things going on in my life; what with the playground, the friends and the playleaders who really looked out for us. There were about thirty kids that grew up together in those flats and, you know, we were a happy bunch of kids. We were always acting, dancing, singing, playing games and, anything else we could think of to have fun, we did it. The playleaders were great and they helped us out in every way they could. Everything for us kids revolved around the playground in the flats. Even the shed was used when it came to birthday parties and our mas thought this was great. Parents would allow their kids to have their parties down there. When it was my cousin's birthday, my aunt sent down a beautiful big cake. She picked it out, she said, from a shop window because it looked so nice. It was covered in icing so off she sent it with the rest of the sweets down to the shed to Lady Reilly who was in charge of the playground at that time.

But when she started to cut the cake it just collapsed in on itself. There was no inside to the cake. The icing was wrapped around a circular piece of cardboard. It was only in the shop window for show and as well as that it was actually a wedding cake. Well, Lady Reilly went mad and shouted up to my auntie, *"Mrs Burke, do you think this is funny?"* Well, I don't know to this day how she got hold of it but anyway we knew better than to go asking questions My aunt thought it was funny herself but she told Lady Reilly she hadn't a clue how that had happened. The shop must have made a mistake! My ma says that the reason most birthday parties took place in the playground was because the mothers didn't want to get their flats dirty.

Even though the ladies were great with us and helped in every way they could, at the same time they allowed us to make a lot of our own choices, which was just as well because I always had my own mind. But they corrected you when you were wrong and sometimes they actually stopped you from coming into the playground if you were bold enough. There was many a time that I was stopped. I guess I always said how I felt and it didn't always go down too well. But at the end of the day we had great respect for the leaders and always remembered them when it came to buying presents. I felt they deserved a lot because they gave a lot. I remember the day we went in for a big talent competition over in the St Francis Xavier Hall on Merchant's Quay. We sang the old song 'Do you want your old lobby washed down?' We hadn't a clue what it meant but, boy, we worked very hard for that competition and won first prize. We were so proud of ourselves. Because we did so well and because she was so proud of us our playleader Helena Lynch, decided to write into *The Late Late Show*. We went for several auditions and finally we were accepted to appear on the *Toy Show*. One of the songs we were to sing had the words 'Son of the Father' and with us coming from the inner city, of course, we pronounced it 'Son of Dee Fader'. An elocution teacher was brought in to the studio to try and help us pronounce it properly as it was driving the producer mad. But they gave up and said that there was no hope of us getting it right for television that night. Now back then you really had to be posh to be on television and you had to pronounce your words properly. Luckily our playleader, Helena, believed in us and it didn't matter to her that we couldn't pronounce the words. We tried all day and night and the producers were going round in a daze. Helena knew everything would work out just fine as it always did. So it came to the final moment and Helena was strumming her guitar and hoping that we would get it right. As those words approached we pronounced them perfectly. Helena was bursting with pride and delight that she had believed in us from day one and we made her proud. We were to appear on the *Toy Show*. This was a really big deal because we were from the inner city and inner-city kids didn't appear on television too often in those years. People sometimes thought that because you were from the inner city that you were less important and that was very wrong. The afternoon that we went out to the television studio in Donnybrook a private bus pulled up outside the flats to pick us up. We were just so excited. There were twenty-two of us who went on that show. We were all allowed to wear our Christmas clothes that day so it was a great feeling. All the

mothers gathered outside the flats to wave us off and they
were crying with happiness.

"*Ah, Jesus, our kids, look at them. They're like movie
stars.*"

I swear it was funny. You would think we were going
to Hollywood. Well, I guess it felt like that to them. I was
eleven then and a very proud eleven-year-old. We spent
the whole day out in R.T.É. We were brought to the
canteen in the studio and we spotted Gay Byrne for the
first time. This was before satellite channels and MTV so
he was the nearest thing to a star that we had. We were
disappointed that we didn't get to chat to him because he
was busy but, anyway, just catching sight of him made me
happy. After a long day rehearsing we appeared on the
Toy Show that night and sang two songs, our winning
song 'Do you want your old lobby washed down?' and,
of course, since it was Christmas and the toy show, we
sang 'O come all ye faithful'. I will always remember that
song because when we were on the stage I looked over at
the television screen and who was looking back at me
only myself, as clear as day. I felt really special because
my face was on the screen all on its own. Another thing I
will never forget about that night was that when we came
home our mothers were so proud of us. That will stay
with me forever. Their expressions said everything. A few
weeks later Gay Byrne sent us out a cheque for sixty
pounds (to the leaders in the playground) and he also gave
us six guitars. This was brilliant because out of that money
the twenty-two of us went on a weekend away to Cavan.

* * *

My parents – Martha and Harry Cahill

That's me and my father, with my sister Miriam on the right

My sister Diane's Communion – me on the right, my sister Miriam
on the left – matching dresses again!

All the family at Butlins in the 1970's

Butlins in the 70's: that's me, number 88, with cousin Tammy on the left and my cousin Lisa and sister Miriam on the right

My First Holy Communion – a proud day for my family

"Lobby Washed Down" from *The Late, Late Show* – some of the girls from the flats

The Sound of Music rehearsal before our performance at the Tudor Rooms: me – back row, fourth from left, with the rest of the girls from the flats

All Ireland Disco Dancing Champions – check out the outfits!

Meeting the Lord Mayor with my trophy – that's me front row, first right

SWINGING!

• Two swinging girls with plenty to smile about! For both
have won weekly heats of the Swingers Dance competition,
organised by Mosney Holidays in association with
SUNDAY WORLD and Sony.
    Left: Janet Cohel of Moyclare Close, Baldoyle, Dublin,

Famous at last – making it into the papers for winning a dance competition

Selling Christmas wrapping paper – that's me on the right, Anita behind me

Girls' Blackpool trip – that's me in the red jumper

Looking glamorous: left to right – my mother, Paul, me and my
mother's friend Jean, before Paul and I go to the Debs

Years later when I worked in Londis supermarket I used to have all the girls in the canteen with the brushes and their mops singing 'Do you want your old lobby washed down?'. The owner, Mr. O'Sullivan, would come into the canteen and laugh at us and just raise his head up to the sky. So I carried all my joys of the 'lobby washed down' even into my adult life.

8

Kilnacrott Abbey was owned by the Norbertine order for many years but in 1977 they passed it over to the North Inner-City Community. This was wonderful for all the children in the inner city as a cheap holiday in a wonderful place. Costs are kept as low as possible with a week's stay costing between sixty and one hundred euros depending on the funds available for the kids. The main house holds about thirty people but today they have an extra two cottages which can hold up to thirty kids. There is every possible activity available for the kids with indoor basket ball, volley ball and football, sailing, canoeing, archery, BMX courses and ordinary bikes for leisure trips. It all happened here for us all those years ago on our long weekend-away trip to celebrate our appearance on *The Late Late Show*. Our playleader, Helena Lynch, who was only in her twenties at the time brought all twenty-two of us away that weekend. Looking back now it was very brave of her to take that trip on.

Living in the city the nights were never very dark so in Cavan the most exciting part of the weekend was the darkness of the night. We would go for midnight walks and everywhere would be pitch black. We would call out to one another, 'Where are you?', 'Over here' and with that we would all hold on to each other tightly because the fear of God would be in us. We even ventured on walks through the graveyard in the dead of night just to terrify ourselves, and sometimes Helena would jump out on us, frighten the living daylights out of us and keep us in order. We all slept in the same room and one night the ladies who were in charge were cooking chickens for dinner. The next day we all sneaked down to the kitchen and robbed two chickens, brought them back up to the room and ate them with a few drinks. I remember Diane saying to me, "Jenna, take a sup." I did and then she said to me, "Now if you squeal on me I'll squeal on you," so I guess she had me on that one. But she would probably tell you that I was always squealing on her.

It was the last day of our weekend and as it was Sunday we all decided to go to Mass with Helena. Just outside the church there was a shop that sold gifts and holy items. While we were in the church some of the gang left and headed to the gift shop while the rest stayed in the church. One of the lads could not take his eyes off a big glass charity collection bottle stuffed with money, even pound notes and a lot of them. He thought this was just brilliant and wanted those pound notes so badly. He tried to rob the money out of the bottle but there was a big cork stuck in the top so it was hard to get at the money. He got into a fit trying to shake the cork out of the bottle and at this stage he was attracting quite an audience with his colourful language. He was shaking it like mad while the old people in the church watched in amazement. With it being such a rural area they would never have seen the likes of this before, with twenty-two kids running all over the place in different directions. Some of older people just held on tightly to their rosary beads and shook their heads, glancing up to the heavens in the hope that God would just explain what was going on, because they couldn't understand. Poor Helena was on her own trying to deal with the situation inside the church while the rest of the gang were outside in the shop, robbing it blind. Eventually the priest asked Helena to control us but she was doing her best. She stood up and pointing to the shop she suggested that he not waste time and go back to his shop as quick as he could. *"If I were you I would get back into that shop or everything is going to be gone."* Helena was furious. Of course, the young fella still had no luck with the bottle so she left him busy trying to figure out how to get at the money while she headed towards the shop with the priest, there to find some of the girls putting things down their tops and down their trousers. When they realised that the stuff was holy, they took it back out as quickly again and put it back on the shelves. They would never rob 'holy stuff'. The priest couldn't stop thanking Helena in the end for putting him on the right road but he was glad to see the back of us. Poor Helena was in all different directions at one time dealing with so many kids. She had brought a friend with her to help her, but at this stage we were so out of control that her friend gave up. But no, Helena, she was strong and believed in us and knew that soon, even if it was hours later, we would get tired and calm down, and everything would be okay. Helena knew that we were good kids, but we were kids and sometimes we got up to no good but through thick and thin she stayed there and dealt with everything. She just wouldn't give up because she knew there was a lot of goodness inside us.

* * *

With the six guitars from *The Late Late Show*, Helena offered lessons to whoever wanted to learn. I remember my cousin, Anita, and I were dead keen. My ma and da gave me the money to buy my own guitar in Walton's Music Shop in Parnell Square. I was over the moon with myself because Anita also got a new guitar from her ma. Now we were just getting good when a few weeks later Helena told us that she was leaving. Now Helena was the best and we all loved her. She brought light into our lives as we did into hers. She left because she wasn't getting on with one of the other ladies. Oh, my God, we were all just so sad. We thought that it was the end of the world. The day that she left I will never forget. She went home on her bike with us all running after her shouting, *"Helena, don't go. Please, don't go."*

We were all running down Sean MacDermott Street. crying our eyes out. But, she did go and we never saw her again after that. I never played the guitar again.

* * *

While I was writing this book I was reminiscing with my sister Miriam one day and the chat started about Helena and how good she had been to us. I thought how wonderful it would be to find her again and see if her memories were as happy as ours and if we meant as much to her as she did to us. Would I ring a radio show maybe and put out a call for her? But she might not like that sort of publicity. In the end we didn't but still in our hearts we were hoping that one day we would succeed in finding her. Quite coincidentally I bumped into a friend who had bumped into Helena near where she worked. So, this was meant to be. How after all those years could this happen without a reason? Myself and Anita were driving by her place of work and Anita said to me, *"Jenna that's where Helena works."* So that was it! There was no time like the present. I went in and asked for her. It turned out that she wasn't working that day but I left a little note with my phone numbers. Now I wasn't sure if I was going to hear from her but sure enough my mobile rang one morning and it was a message from Helena. I just couldn't believe it; I was just so happy that another dream had come true for me. I called her back and we talked. The first thing I said to her was, *"Have I got the right Helena?"*

"Yes," she said.

I swear I was just over the moon with happiness. *"Helena,"* I said to her, *"you broke our hearts and I mean that in the loveliest way. We all loved you so much."* Helena was crying but very happy about the whole thing. We didn't stay on the phone long as she was in work but she gave me her home number and I called her back that evening. We then talked for a long time and made arrangements to meet. Honest to God, it was a wonderful feeling. I phoned Anita and she had met Helena that day also. Anita was over the moon. So Anita and I made more arrangements and a few phone calls later we had arranged to meet with a few of the girls from the flats from old days and, of course, get together with Helena. This was quite an achievement as it was twenty-five years since we had all been together. Helena was the most nervous as she thought we had all changed so much. On the phone I had said that I had gone to America and was getting a divorce and that I didn't drink and that Anita wouldn't be drinking either so we could give her a lift home (Anita was pregnant and that is why she wasn't drinking). Helena said that she would bring her guitar now as kids we would rarely have seen Helena without her guitar.

Well, the night finally came. Oh, I just couldn't wait but I was nervous at the same time My ma and Miriam came along, of course, as well. We laughed and got talking like old times straight away but I noticed that Helena did not have her guitar with her. *"Helena where is your guitar?"*

"Jenna, when I was talking to you on the phone and you told me that you didn't drink and Anita didn't drink and you had lived in America for seventeen years I thought that you were all born again Christians or something so I didn't know what to expect and I never brought the guitar." We all laughed. Helena was her old self and had never changed. She went back home for her guitar. We had a brilliant night singing all the old songs and new songs in the lobby of the Grand Hotel. Passers-by just had to stop and listen to Helena's singing as she was so good. Our other playleader, Carol, was there too and it was the

first time we had ever seen Helena and Carol together. We learned a lot about them that night and we never realised when we were kids that they were friends outside our lives and we never knew. We were happy to see both of them and to hear all the stories about the playground. It turned out that Carol lives not too far from Anita and Helena works in the same area and lives not too far from my ma. So, after all these years, she only lived about a five-minute drive from us. The emotions were strong that night as Helena and Carol told of how great those years were for them and that they had truly never met people like us again. But now we are reunited and we will never lose contact again. Actually there are plans already to get together with all the girls from the flats on a regular basis.

When Helena left St Joseph's Mansions, Lady Reilly took over. Now I don't know why we called these women 'lady'. I guess it was instilled into us by our parents. Our parents respected them so much and they wanted us to have the same respect for them.

Lady Reilly was really nice. She sometimes came across as being very tough but we knew she really wasn't. She put you out of the playground if you were bold and as I have said I did get put out a couple of times. I tell you if anyone climbed over the railings, straight away she would put you out for the day. But I suppose she had to set limits. One thing she always did, though, was enquire after me if I was sick, which I was a lot. She would shout up to my ma, *"Mrs. Cahill, how is Jenna today?"*

"She's grand, Lady Reilly."

She was kind-hearted and I really liked her.

Another of the playground ladies was Carol Morrissey. Carol was like a little doll. She was beautiful and we all liked her. She wasn't much older than us and she didn't like to be called Lady, because it made her feel too old, so we called her Carol and she became our friend. One time when Carol was saving to go away on holidays, week after week she would buy something nice out of her wages. One particular time she saw a lovely pair of shoes in Simon Hart's shop in Talbot Street. I said to her one day, *"Carol, why are you not getting the shoes?"*

She replied, *"I can't get them this week because I haven't got the money. I'll get them next week."*

So I kept asking her more questions to find out what the sandals looked like. Finally when I realised what she wanted I went over to Fr. Casey in the presbytery and asked him for a note to go around to the shop and get those shoes for her. I can't remember what the note said but you could say that it was a begging note. They gave us the sandals and we brought them back to Carol so that she didn't have to wait to buy them. And any time Carol had no milk for her tea, one of us kids would go over to the shop and steal a bottle of milk for her. There was nothing we would not have done for Carol. The corporation moved the playleaders around to different playgrounds and one day the head man wanted to place Carol somewhere else. When we heard this we all got together and went on strike outside the playground so that we could keep Carol. We had lost Helena so we were not prepared to lose another good lady. We had to put up a fight. They wanted to put two old sisters in her place and we were not having that. They had cars so we threw eggs and flour over the cars to put them off staying with us. It worked. In the end Carol stayed with us, thank God. She did loads of plays with us and made sure we practised. But we didn't just do plays; we got involved in any sport that we could play around where we lived also. We even had basketball teams in town and there would be girls from all the surrounding flats on the same team. Most of the girls living in Sean Tracey's flats were on Diane's team (Sean Tracey flats were straight across from St Joseph's Mansions, just out the back gate). My sister Diane hung around with the girls from Sean Tracey's flats. I remember one night sitting on the stairs when they were all planning to go on gore. 'Gore' was a slang word for running away from home. Diane didn't want me to go so she sent me home. I guess because I always squealed on her I spoiled it for myself. Anyway she told me afterward that they stayed on the stairs all night but she told my ma that she stayed in her friend's house. What was wrong with all of us girls? We always wanted to run away. I guess at that age we were probably looking for attention and we thought that was a good way to get it.

* * *

Well, we got plenty of attention in 1979 when Pope John Paul 11 came to Ireland. During his trip to Ireland he was due to visit Matt Talbot's tomb in Sean MacDermott Street Church and our school choir was to sing for him. Well, this was a huge deal. The people living in town were very religious and loved the Pope. All the flats around Joseph's Mansions, Liberty House, Mary's Mansion's,

Lourdes Flats, and all the other surrounding flats got together to clean the whole neighbourhood especially for the Pope. Everywhere around the inner city the pillars and the path edges were painted yellow and white, the Papal colours. All the children wore yellow and white for the day of his arrival. It was just like getting dressed up for St Patrick's Day only this time everybody was in yellow and white instead of green. There were flags hanging out every window and off every lamppost that day and the streets were decorated with yellow and white bunting. The whole of town was hopping. People were out from early morning; the older ones taking their chairs with them ready for the long wait.

With everyone being so excited, the priest even went to the extremes of putting up big screens in the church for all the old people as most of them wouldn't be able to make it to the Phoenix Park for the Mass. Even a BBC television crew was waiting in the church for the Pope's arrival. The church was packed with the elderly and the organisers had laid out tables down the aisle of the church and put lunch for all the elderly. This would make the day even more memorable. No one else was allowed into the church. With a band playing outside, the happiness of the people that day was never forgotten. Everybody was very patient as the Pope was extremely late. It would be hours before the Pope arrived but from early morning people started to arrive, anxious to get a place in the grounds of the church because they thought that the Pope was going to go into the church. The way they looked at it: the closer to the Pope, the closer to God. But unfortunately he didn't go into the church that day as he was running late and did not have enough time. All the people in the church grounds grabbed their chairs and ran outside with them to get as close to the Pope as possible especially the older people. I remember watching the Popemobile going down Sean MacDermott Street. It had bullet-proof glass in the windows and I swear I can see him now and the way he waved at everyone. He gave us his blessing as he passed though. One of the songs that we sang for him was 'Céad Míle Fáilte, Holy Father to Ireland, we welcome you with our dear smile'. That song will always stick in my mind.

Though his visit was short it left a huge impression on the inner city. Any boy that was born after the Pope's visit was named John Paul and all you would hear down in the flats was, *"John Paul, come up for your dinner."* Now there was also a play being staged during his visit called *Kips, Digs and Villages'*. The play was based on the Pope coming to visit Sean MacDermott Street and one of the lines that was inserted after his visit was "Here he comes and there he fucking goes!" The play was about all the build-up for the Pope and the effort that the people put in for him and the fact that he was in and out of Sean MacDermott Street in I guess you could say minutes. He headed for the Phoenix Park where he said a Mass for people from the whole of Ireland who came to see him and to attend that Mass that day. Later the Pope's office sent the priest in Sean MacDermott Street a letter thanking him so much. I found out later the reason the Pope never stopped was because the police thought that it wasn't safe enough because by now there were a lot of vacant flats around. They felt that the opportunity was there, if anyone wanted to get a shot at the Pope, just to go into one of the flats. One of the priests of our parish was very angry about this. He was a member of the Portmarnock Golf Club and he felt that the poor had been let down.

He just said, *"The hell with them all"* and he never played golf again. He looked on golf as a rich man's game so he couldn't support it again for that reason. Later Fr. Lemass and Fr. Lavelle, the two priests of our parish, headed out for a pint after that big day to recover.

Now as I said people in the inner city were very religious and all the old people in particular had a devotion to some saint or other. The Legion of Mary had their big day in May when a procession was held to celebrate the feast of Our Lady.

I suppose for us this procession marked the beginning of summer and all of our outdoor activities. The people all worked together to make sure everywhere was spotless. Windows and door knockers had to be cleaned and polished to within an inch of their lives for this day and in the garden of St Joseph's Mansions a statue of Our Lady with white stones surrounding it was erected every May. This was a very special day particularly for the communion girls. They would all put their communion dresses on and together with the adults they would process all the way up Killarney Street to Sean MacDermott Street. Hundreds of people took part in the procession through the streets which this time were decorated with blue and white bunting. Some of the adults even wore blue capes around their shoulders in honour of Our Lady. As the procession took place we children sang *"Ave Maria, Ave Maria,"* and for this day all the older women would bring their rosary beads to the church to get them blessed by the priest. Even the teachers from Rutland Street School would make their way to the church just to be there that day. I always thought as a child that the people in town were very holy because I remember as a kid if you let a sweet drop on the ground you were always told to bless it before you ate it. If you didn't bless it, then it was thought that the devil had spat on it. I tell you, you never dreamt of eating it until you blessed it because you never wanted the devil near you.

9

The arrival of summer meant that soon we would be going on holiday to Sunshine House in Balbriggan, north County Dublin. This was one of the highlights of my childhood. From the early days of summer down in the yard of the flats we would all be asking one another, *"Who do you think is going to Sunshine House this year?"* To be honest you had to have no money to go there and each year we would apply in the hope that we would be the lucky ones. One year we were dead lucky and eight of us cousins got to go at one time. We were waved off on the train by our families from Connolly Station. I know we were only going to the coast north of Dublin but for us kids we might as well have been going to Africa. Anywhere outside the city was like a foreign country and seemed like miles away. We were laden down with sweets to eat on the journey in case we starved and as if we didn't know when we were going to get our next meal.

When we arrived we headed with great excitement to see where we would be sleeping. Luckily we all got to share a dormitory called Little Flower and Anita's bed was facing mine. I remember Anita had brought a small tin of Turkish Delight with her which I thought was very exotic. One night I wasn't feeling so good and Anita said to me, *"Jenna, will a piece of Turkish Delight make you better?*

"Yeah, Anita, maybe it will."

I think Anita was just trying to comfort me but whatever it was I felt better almost immediately. I just loved it and I still love it today. The smell and the taste take me straight back to those summers. Being down in Sunshine House was a lot of fun. In the dining-room we would sing at every meal and the singsong always included 'Sweet Molly Malone' of course, and 'One Finger, One Thumb, Keep Moving'. They were great songs. The head lady in the kitchen was called Molly, so we all called her Molly Malone. Back then the summers always seemed to be hot and every day the leaders took us down to the beach where we would take part in all sorts of competitions. The week would just fly by with each day filled with one activity after another. I have to tell you going down to Sunshine House to us was the best holiday in the world.

Another really popular spot was Mosney or Butlins. Everybody went to Mosney at some time in their lives. All of our family went down together; God there must have been about forty of us there one time. We always went during the first week in August. Just like when we were heading for Sunshine House we would all meet up at Connolly Station and get the train down. It was a great feeling. All the cousins, aunts and uncles, mothers and fathers and grannies and granddads would go together and the laughing and joking and chatting would go on for ever. When we reached a certain point on the train journey near Mosney all of us kids would get so excited that we would be jumping up in the air and shouting, *"There's Butlins. There's Butlins. We're nearly there."*

"What do you want to go on first?" one kid would say to the other.

"Ah, I'm going on the bumper cars first."

So we would all be organising our day before we even left the train. All the mas and das would meet up at Dan Lowry's, the most popular pub in Butlins. At night-time, of course, the kids weren't allowed into the pub. There were bouncers at the door but we would try to sneak in anyway. It was very hard because we were always caught and thrown back out. But even that was all part of the holiday. We knew we would be caught but trying to get in was half the fun. Sometimes we would be lucky and when we eventually got inside it was great. We would sit beside our aunts and uncles and they would give us nothing but compliments.

"Isn't she lovely?"

"I think she will be a model when she grows up."

To tell you the truth they said that to every one of us kids and none of us turned out to be models. Another one would say, *"She'll be an actress."*

I swear they never stopped. My granny's maiden name was Crosby so she always told us that Bing Crosby was our uncle and that we would take after him. They actually told a good few lies and we really believed them but it was great for our confidence and as children we felt nothing but loved and admired by all. When Dan Lowry's closed we would wait for our mas and das to come out so they could buy us chips in the café on the way back to the chalet. Sometimes one family would end up in another family's chalet because they would be twisted drunk. They were all mad, but it was great fun and a carefree time for everyone. Now, I have to say there were also a good few fights in Butlins and I'd run for my life if I saw a fight going on. It didn't happen to our family because we all got along great but some families would be at one another hammer and tongs. I suppose they came away together to have a family holiday but then discovered that they actually couldn't stand the sight of one another. It was easy to get drunk in Butlins because nearly everybody went to the pub every night and the drink flowed.

All week long in Butlins there were competitions of all sorts from bonny babies to glamorous grannies. We went in for every competition going. I guess this was what made our holiday even better. Everyone would cheer you on and it didn't matter whether you won or lost; you were still told that you were great. There would always be a talent show, a fancy dress competition and a disco-dancing competition. My favourite was the disco-dancing competition. Though I will never forget the 'Mr. and Mrs.' competition and the year my ma and da went in for it. I was so happy and excited. I loved the idea of my ma and da being in love and seeing them up on the stage showing how much in love they were and how much they knew about each other. I really believed that everyone was looking at them thinking how romantic they were and how lucky a girl I was to have them as my ma and da. I felt very proud of them.

I was a good dancer as a kid and back home in the flats we were always entering competitions. So, when I entered the dancing competition I got first place and a free weekend full board in Mosney. I had to go back to Mosney in the late summer because at the end of the season they had all the winners back and then they picked an overall winner. This time the competition was extremely hard but I still managed to get second prize. I was over the moon and my photograph appeared in the *Sunday World* and that even made it better again. The Redcoats, the helpers, were brilliant at Mosney and so good to all the kids. They played games and danced and sang with us all day and every evening. I think the Redcoats made Butlins a better place. There were also Greencoats. Now, these were different, much more serious and they took care of any fights that might happen. I never had anything to do with them, thank God, and we felt safer having them around the place.

But the one thing I will always remember was the last night when everyone threw each other in the pool. We all got a good laugh out of it and it was a great way to end the holiday. The next day, Saturday, was going home day and everybody wore a miserable expression when they got up that morning. Nobody liked going home and not even the thought of the return train journey could brighten our mood. A cloud came over the place, as far as we were concerned, until we came back the next year.

Down through all the years, ever since I was a kid, Butlins still holds marvellous memories for the next generation of our family until just five years ago when some of our family went back to Butlins to experience the magic once again. There must have been twenty of us in the chalet that weekend. There were bodies everywhere and I tell you the place was so old that it was mouldy. Butlins wasn't the same for me any more. It just wasn't like years ago, but the kids still loved it. The one thing that bothered me was the kids still wanted to wander around on their own and Jonathan wanted to go with them, of course, but I had changed. The carefree days of my childhood were long gone. I was now a mother and all I could see were the dangers that lay all around. While all the kids ran excitedly about the place, I was following at a safe distance pretending to be out for a walk. Well, my nerves were just gone. There I was hiding behind walls making sure they were okay and at the same time trying to give Jonathan a bit of freedom. I know when we were small we were allowed to wander around Butlins on our own but times had changed. I had been living in America and children were not given the same amount of freedom as the kids in Ireland. I only lasted in Butlins two days that week. I just had enough and there were too many people in one chalet for me. I guess I wasn't used to crowds staying in one room any more after being in America for so long. I headed back to Dublin that day deciding that the best thing for me was to cherish my childhood memories of long-ago summers.

Strangely enough it was the simple week spent in Sunshine House that held its wonder when I visited a couple of years ago.

It was a beautiful day in July of 2004 and Anita and her kids had come down to our house in Balrothery. We were sitting outside chatting over a sup of tea as usual but the kids had us tormented. They wanted us to take them out for a trip. I swear I wasn't really in the mood but, you know as always, we gave into the kids and took them out to a fun park at Bettystown in County Meath. The kids had a blast. We were on our way back at about 7 o'clock and decided to go into the hotel in Balbriggan for dinner. We were sitting down chatting away over dinner when Anita said to me, *"Jenna, where is Sunshine House from here?"*

"God, Anita, it's literally two minutes around the corner. Do you want to go around?"

"Ah, Jenna, it's late. We'll leave it for another day."

"No, Anita, come on and we'll show the kids."

When the kids had finished their meal we headed around to Sunshine House. Jonathan and I headed straight up to the door and knocked not knowing what to expect.

"Hi, my name is Jenna and when I was a little girl I came here. My friend is with me. She also came here as a kid and we were wondering could we come in and visit."

The president of Sunshine House happened to be there that day and the man who answered the door headed off to fetch him. Not before he invited us to come in, of course. He was very welcoming and Anita and all her gang came in. We met with the president of Sunshine House and we stood in the hallway talking about how we remembered it as kids and how much we loved it there. It brought back great memories for Anita and me. Our kids loved it too. Nothing much had changed although the dormitories had new beds. Outside besides the main building there was a new building with loads of different rooms. The room that our kids loved most of all was the playroom which had fun-ball pools to jump into and a climbing wall. The kids were told they could take off their shoes and play. This really made their day. There was also a karaoke room and a computer room. Twenty-five years later I just felt like a kid again. It felt so good that our kids didn't want to leave. There must have been something magical about Sunshine House because, despite the fact that our kids have so much, that basic house in Balbriggan could cause such happiness, smiling faces and gut-wrenching laughs among children well used to holidays of all sorts. And how nice it was that the staff at Sunshine House still had that welcoming approach towards all children and on that particular day to a couple of big kids who were happy to head down Memory Lane just one more time.

10

Across the road from St Joseph's Mansions was Buckingham Street where the Sisters of Charity ran the 'stew house', as it was known around the city. The nuns were very kind to everyone who found themselves in a bit of bother financially. They never asked questions or judged those who needed their help. Almost anyone could find themselves at the stew house as many of the inner-city dwellers lived very close to poverty. Any small change in a family's circumstances would find them on the bread line. The nuns provided a hot meal every day between 10am and 12.30pm each day of the year. I remember people in the flats would talk about families that had to go there. They were always on the lookout to see which family had fallen on hard times. We were lucky because we never had to go to the stew house, but living could become very hard very quickly in the inner city. Anita and I used to take care of kids whose mammy was an alcoholic. There were four kids in that family and Anita's ma, Mary, was really good to them. Their mother turned an alcoholic when her husband committed suicide and she wasn't able to cope with life. She was a nice lady though and was never abusive to her children. Life was tough but people had their own children and their own lives and they couldn't always be there for everyone else. Only for Anita's ma they would have been lost but sometimes when there was no one taking care of them Anita and I would step in and do our best. And not to mention that we were only kids ourselves. But saying that, this was the way we were brought up, to help others.

When times got very hard some people had to pawn their jewellery and clothes if they had no money. I remember my ma would put her wedding ring in the pawn and a few weeks later when she had enough money she would pay to get it back. She did this many times, and many more families did the same. My ma remembers seeing children's communion clothes and father's good suits being pawned. Well, thank God for the pawn back then, or we would have gone hungry. But if my ma hadn't got any money sometimes my granny would try to help us out.

Though times could be hard and money was often short, my ma and her friends knew how to have a good time. They were the best laugh altogether and I have some great memories. My da often came in from work to find my ma and her friends up dancing. The table would be put up on top of the couch and there they would be doing rock-'n'-roll. They were brilliant dancers. Coming up to the flats you would hear 'One o'clock, two o'clock, three o'clock, rock' day after day. My da never said anything; he always just smiled. They would be throwing each other over their shoulders and they had all the moves. This went on day after day. Every Sunday night they would go to Molly Malone's down by Smithfield markets and they would enter competitions. I remember standing down in the yard of the flats when they would be going out. I was very proud of my ma because she always looked beautiful. I thought she was the best-looking woman in St. Joseph's Mansions. She was just a great mother and always did her best for us. In fact my ma is a very good person to everyone who comes to her for help. She never hesitates but is there for them first-hand. When we lived in the flats, everyone was into the gold names jewellery and I remember my ma buying them for everyone. Well, when I say everyone I mean Miriam, Diane, Anita, Margaret and Vanessa and, of course, me. She worked very hard and spent all her money on everyone else. All you would hear her say was, *"I'll buy you one next week"* or *"I'll leave off one for you."* She made sure we never went without. We were always in fashionable clothes. She would buy lovely dresses for me and Miriam and she would dress us like twins, but I didn't mind this at all. She worked in Marlboro St School as a cleaner in the morning and back again in the evening. My da always worked as well. He was a painter, but when we lived in the flats he never worked Sundays or Mondays. Back then Monday was a day for the pub for all the men. Then the following morning you would hear him say, *"I'm never drinking again."* He would be

111

dying with a hangover. And, of course, he would go to the priest and take the pledge. But, you know yourself, the next week he was back in the pub again.

* * *

Dancing was a big thing in all our lives not just the adults'. We lived for it. Sure, I remember one day in my aunt's house, that's Anita's ma, I was sitting on a chair outside the scullery when out she came carrying three big Irish breakfasts in her hands. There I was dancing away but only using my hands when up in the air went the three breakfasts. She nearly killed me.

"You bleeding eejits, ye! I'm sick of you kids dancing, dancing, and dancing. That's all you do." She was mad with me that day. I was a little bit afraid of her but in a good way. She taught us good manners and they always meant a lot to me and for a while I even lived with them. Sometimes I would organise for all of us kids to get together and do bob-a-jobs to earn some money for our dancing costumes. Every Sunday there were dancing competitions all over Dublin. Many of them were held in the Crofton Airport Hotel. One year we did so well that we made it to the All-Ireland Disco-Dancing Competition. I will never forget standing there waiting for the results to be called out. They started off with fifth place, then fourth place, then third place. When third place was called out the others thought we had no chance so they decided to go and get changed. I didn't because I still had hope. With that they called second place and then they announced that first place went to St. Joey's. Oh, my God! I just

remember leaping over the people in front of me. We were all jumping around with excitement. When we got back home in the van, we drove all around the flats beeping the horn and holding the trophy out the window, All the neighbours came out screaming and shouting, "*Hurray, hurray.*" I swear it was such a great feeling.

We were never bored as kids because when we weren't dancing we were practising our plays. The first play we ever did was *The Sound of Music.* We picked the parts by auditioning in front of each other and then amongst ourselves we would pick the best person for the part. We entered a competition and won first place. Because we were so good we were asked to go to the Tudor Rooms and put that play on as a cabaret. That was a good night. Then we put on the *Wizard of Oz.* This was another great success. Now for this play we were only on stage for five minutes, so we had to do our best. I played the part of Dorothy and once again we won first place.

I tell you as a bunch of kids together we always did very well in our performances because we put in so much practice. We often went down to the Old Folks' Home to put our shows on for the old people. I think this made their day. The people in the inner city always helped the old folks. I remember my ma telling us to go in and clean for an old lady who lived next door to us at 11B. Diane and I used to go in to help her a lot. I swear sometimes the poor woman would send us over to the shop to buy messages and if they came to, say, two pounds, she would often only have given us fifty pence so we used to go home to get the rest from my ma. Then at night my ma would bring her into our house and she would watch television with us. One time my ma was offered money by the government to look after the old lady but she refused. She said that she wasn't doing a job; she was simply taking care of a neighbour. Next door to her lived Lily. Lily was very sick and always had the doctor over to her. So her sister May would knock on our door and ask my ma if I could clean the stairs for the doctor. *"Ah, no problem, May. Jenna will do that when she comes up."* I would get the deck brush and scrub the stairs with disinfectant so that they always smelled good for the doctor. When May asked me to clean the stairs for her, this always made me feel very special and gave me confidence. She made me feel like there was no one else that could do a better job. Next to Lily and May there was Jean, my ma's friend. I remember as a kid going into Jean and asking her would she teach me the capital cities of each country and she was willing to do it. Jean's flat was always a very cosy home to visit because she would have a big coal fire burning every night. She had no problem getting her hands on plenty of coal because this is what her husband did for a living and I loved sitting close to the fire, rattling off my capital cities. You always knew when Jean was coming into our flat because she wore flip-flops and you could hear her flip-flopping up to the door.

In the flats there were a couple of families whose parents were alcoholics. I remember one day the kids in one family were left on their own and Anita and I went up to the flat to mind them. They were filthy so we washed them and put clean clothes on them. I was so happy to be able to help them. Then we went around to the cake shop in Talbot St. and bought the stale cakes so we could give the kids something to eat. We just did our best and exactly what our mothers would have done. There was another family and, Jesus, I remember the kids going down to the gate every evening to carry their mother and father up the stairs. I tell you even as a kid I felt sorry for those kids but my ma always said that those kids would turn out great and the last I heard they had done very well for themselves. I suppose they were learning how to survive in life the hard way. There was always something going on in one flat or another to keep your interest as a child. I remember another day when the ambulance was called to the flats for an elderly man. When the ambulance crew went into the flat to bring the old man out he was sitting in a chair stark naked. All he kept repeating was, *"Jesus came into this world naked and I am going out of this world naked."* The poor man, the neighbours all came together to look after him.

* * *

In hard times too Anita, Miriam, Margaret and I used to go up to the Tuggers off Parnell Street on a Saturday to sell our old clothes. I don't know how it got its name but anyway this was where people brought their spare clothes and laid them out on the street on a Saturday morning. I tell you this was a great way to make money. I was always thinking of ways to make money, but, I hardly ever kept any for myself; I was thinking of my ma and da. Anyway I remember selling on the hill as some locals used to call it. When we went to the Tuggers we would put the clothes in bags and carry them in a pram or trolley or whatever we had that had wheels, as long as we got there. We would arrive about eight o'clock, but the travellers would have been there since five o'clock. They sold linoleum and carpet. Today the Tuggers are divided up into individual spaces and when the old-timers are there and see the young ones coming along they don't like it at all. We weren't desperate for money but you would always be looking out for anyone that you knew there. If you were caught buying on the Tuggers, this wasn't good because the kids would make fun of you. Now I have to admit that even Anita, Miriam, Margaret and I would have our own little talk if we saw someone buying second-hand clothes. But now looking back I thank God that it was there for poor people. Now we weren't mean to anyone, but we were kids and kids do those things sometimes. Sometimes we would get killed because we would have taken clothes to sell that we shouldn't have. It was funny because we would have sold an item for a pound or fifty pence and, Jesus, the piece of clothing probably cost about fifty pounds. After our morning's work we would go back to Anita's place and get washed and dressed and go up town to buy something nice to wear.

My Aunt Betty's children that my mother took in as her own: clockwise from centre – Roslyn, Nicola, Alan, Carly and Leonda

My Aunt Betty

"Drugs left us without a Ma – we love and miss her every day" - Nicola

Sunning ourselves in Cape Cod – left to right: Maureen, Caroline and me

Harvard Square Boston – Caroline, Maureen and me

Holiday of a lifetime – relaxing in the Caribbean with Paul and Jonathan

Our dream trip as a family

Paul and me in LA – spot the famous Hollywood sign

From *The Sound of Music* to Universal Studios!

Me and my son Jonathan

My sister Diane and her husband Niall – the limousine I surprised them with for their honeymoon

Left to right: me, Jonathan, Justin, Anita, with Rhonda behind

On the Empire State Building: left to right – Rhonda, Jonathan, me, Anita and Justin

Me today: happy and content in Ireland

Photograph© Edmund Ross

11

Hallowe'en in the inner city started around September when you would see all the young fellas going around looking for wood or old furniture and tyres. Tyres were very popular as they made a great fire with lots of smoke. They would do this until the night of Hallowe'en and there was a great competition in town to see who could build the biggest bonfire. They would go off around some of the other flats to check how big the opposition's bonfires were. Sometimes you would even see a stolen car in the bonfire. We always had our bonfire with Sean Tracey Flats in an open field between the two flats. The little kids went around all the balconies collecting but we thought we were very smart and we never went out collecting on Hallowe'en night because everyone went out that night and you would make no money. Later we would go around knocking at the doors and shouting, *"Help the Hallowe'en party."* We got fruit at the doors, never sweets like nowadays. If someone gave you a sweet you would think they were rich. We dressed up but I tell you there were no fancy costumes bought. We wore our ma's clothes or costumes we had used in one of our plays and, of course, we put loads of make-up on. Then all the kids would walk around to Busáras on Amien's Street and into some of the local pubs to get help for the Hallowe'en party. One person would go ahead into the pub and check it out. Then they reported back to us, *"Jaysus, this one is packed. We'll make loads of money in here."* Then someone else would go into another pub and would just say, *"Don't even bother going in there. That's empty."* We did this for the whole month of Hallowe'en and if you were lucky you collected lots of money. We were about nine or ten when we were allowed to do this. Any younger and the older kids wouldn't let you go with them. They would say to you, *"If we have to run from the knackers, you will get us all caught."*

"I swear I won't get you caught. Please let me go." Sometimes the little ones would cry but there was nothing you could do. They weren't coming with us and that was it. We always stuck together as a group and never went anywhere without each other. At the end of the night we would go back to the flats to count our money and sometimes we put our money together and shared it out evenly. I tell you we could make about ten pounds a night. All I thought about was that I could buy my own clothes for Christmas and my ma and da wouldn't have to buy them. Well this was my intention but my ma always bought them. I always had a business head on me. Sometimes a gang of us would put on costumes and go around the local pubs and put little acts on for the people. They just

loved this, and we gave them great entertainment. And of course, a hat would be passed around at the end.

Entertainment and entertaining were a big part of our lives and any opportunity for a bit of craic we jumped at it. There used to be a day especially dedicated to children called 'National Children's Day'. We loved this day and early as possible we would head up to O'Connell Street where all the action was taking place. There was a parade and a funfair and thousands of people would gather. One year I was there with all my friends from town when this man came up to us and asked if he could take our photograph. Of course, we were all delighted and we said yes. He asked for our address so I gave him mine. He came to our house and met my ma, and I tell you for a long time my ma couldn't get rid of him. So she hired him to take photographs of all of us. He was a great photographer but I think he was kind of cheeky. On one particular occasion he was in our house and my ma said to me, *"There's your dinner"* and he sat in at the table and said. *"Thanks."* It was kind of funny but he ate all my dinner. I wouldn't mind but my ma had just made him sandwiches and tea before that. Now he was okay but thinking back he could have been anyone that I gave my address to. The parade was always great and I remember when all of us kids from the playground took part in it one year. We made hats. Now when I say 'hats', I mean HATS that came right over our whole bodies. Kids from playgrounds all around our area and from playgrounds all around Dublin, north and south, took part in that parade. I kept the photo that the man took of us that day and later when I was writing to New York for an au pair job I sent that photo of me with the letter. I never heard back, but to be honest I was only about sixteen so I obviously looked too young to be an au pair. But even though I loved the cosiness of living in the inner city with my world all around me in that small area I was always looking to distant shores. I knew that one day I was going to live in America . . .

I suppose I was always looking outward to another way of life and always interested in other people's lives. Sometimes when we stayed in my Aunt Jenny's house, Anita and I would get up in the middle of the night and go down to the Gresham Hotel just to sit in the bathroom or powder room as it was called. Looking back I can now see that it was actually a very dangerous thing to do but there was something exotic and interesting in that place and the women who would go in and out of the powder room, reapplying their make-up and fixing their hair. The Gresham Hotel was literally only about ten minutes from Anita's house. After that we would head up to the twenty-four-hour shop on the North Circular Road and buy something to eat. Now if we did this we would go down the next morning to Anita's ma and da and tell them that Jenny's kids kept us awake all night and we couldn't sleep. So Skinner would say to us *"Get into bed and I'll make you a bowl of porridge and some toast."* He made such a fuss over us and if he really knew what we had been up to he would probably have killed us.

* * *

Christmas time in the flats was homely, cosy and magical

and another opportunity for celebration and fun in our lives. The preparations and excitement brought a lovely warm feeling to my stomach. God, I remember those Christmases well. Christmas morning was always manic. I remember looking over the balcony at all the kids on their new bikes, flying around the four blocks. This was safe to do as at that time there were hardly any cars in the flats. The girls would be playing with their dolls and prams and the boys would have their toy soldiers, bikes and guns at the ready for a great game as soon as the friends came out to play. This was a colourful spectacle. My granny always made the Christmas pudding. The turkey and ham came prepared to perfection with pineapple and cherries on top and cooked. My ma got the whole works from a shop in Fairview. And, Jesus, she must have bought about ten large pans of bread, several tins of biscuits and giant slabs of cake. I tell you the food was never-ending. Christmas Eve was very special because, like all kids, we wouldn't be able to wait for Santa to come. And down in the flats, God, for the longest time, at least a month before Christmas, all you would hear is, *"What are you getting off Santee?"* And I tell you even the adults would ask you. On Christmas Eve we finally got our Christmas tree up. That was the moment we couldn't wait for. We always got so excited about putting the tinsel and lights on the tree and then, finally, the last decoration, the angel, was put on top. Christmas was here. I think we were the last family to get the tree up. I have to say even to this day our house is always hectic on Christmas Eve. There's never a dull moment. My brothers and sisters and I would wake up at about five o'clock on

Christmas morning to see what Santa had brought us and to eat our selection boxes. We never ate breakfast because we would be full of chocolate. My ma always bought new bedclothes for the beds and new night-dresses, pyjamas, slippers and housecoats. Oh, of course, the most important thing about Christmas morning was going to Mass in your new clothes. Everyone got Mass on Christmas morning and my da always made sure of that. My ma redecorated our whole house every year, just for Christmas. She still does it and there is a race to finish it for the big day, but she always gets it done. I loved this as a child because we all helped as a family. God, I remember moving furniture around with my da while my ma gave the instructions as to where she wanted everything to go. One year my da was painting and Anita and I were moving furniture and, Jesus, the tin of paint fell all over the new carpet. Anita did that one but we forgave her because she was helping out. Down in the yard of the flats on Christmas morning the questions would start in earnest, *"What did you get off Santee?"* *"Look what I got."* *"Oh, my God, that's brilliant."* *"You got that? God you're lucky."*

Then you would hear some of the bigger kids saying, *"I got twenty pound, because I'm too big for toys."* *"Can I have a shot of your bike?"* *"Ahh, can I see your doll?"* All of our cousins used to come into our flat on Christmas evening and sometimes they would stay for nearly a week. We would all watch the Christmas films together. I really loved Elvis movies. I don't know why, but they just made my Christmas. And then there would be a singsong and mighty craic the whole night long. One of the most exciting parts of Christmas was Funderland held every year at the R.D.S. It seemed like the whole of Dublin went there at least one day over Christmas. The only thing about the fair though, was that it cost a fortune. So any money your aunts or uncles gave you for Christmas was spent at Funderland. All the excitement of Christmas in the flats went on for at least two weeks until after what we called 'Old Christmas Day', the 6th of January. And then according to tradition in our family we went to visit our cousins.

Coming up to Christmas time when we were a bit older we would sell in Henry Street. I used to sell wrapping paper, with Anita and we used to put our money in together. I have to say we made a lot of money. This made me very happy because I didn't have to ask my ma for money for clothes for Christmas. I bought my own and had my own spending money. I was also able to give her a few bob for herself. I always thought of my mother and father, because I knew they gave us everything they could possibly give us. When I was growing up I wasn't really ever into going out much, but always thought about getting ahead and making something of my life. But we had some of our best laughs selling in Henry Street . . . *"Get your wrapping paper, five sheets for twenty." "Will I give ye five sheets there, love?"* I never allowed anyone to walk by me unless they bought at least five sheets and then they would say to me, *"Jaysus, you're a great saleswoman."*

Our place to sell was just outside Roche's Stores, right in front of the main doors. Sometimes the doorman would tell us to go away, and sometimes we actually had to run, especially when we saw the police coming because only the people who had the stalls had a traders' licence, and we had none. We would go upstairs to Roche's Stores' café for our lunch and on a cold December day that was definitely the best part of the day. I always got a hot bowl of oxtail soup and a bread roll. Sometimes, if it was a busy day, Anita and I would take turns for lunch breaks. If I took a long time I swear she would go mad but she used to make me laugh when she got mad at me. The thing was that we were always best friends so we could get mad at each other and then be friends again. I just loved Christmas in Dublin especially around four o'clock when the lights came on in Henry Street and the carol singers were out. I swear it was just a great feeling, a homely feeling, where everyone knew each other. A lot of the girls from the surrounding flats also had their spots on Henry Street so it brought us even closer and helped us to maintain our friendships as we became older and moved away from the games that once brought us together. *"How are ya? Did ya sell much today?"*

"Ah, about two bales,"

"Jaysus, that wasn't bad at all."

"How did you do?"

"OK, can't complain. It puts the dinner on the table for the kids and gets them their few clothes and toys for Christmas."

I swear you would hear some of the dealers giving out at the top of their voices, *"Here I am, out slaving while that fucking bastard is in the pub all day."* I would just laugh at them because they weren't really serious. It was just part of the street banter and we thought the craic was ninety. On the way home to my aunt's house, Anita and I would go into the Kylemore for a cup of tea and to count our money. We kept a small bag around our necks to keep the money safe and we always made sure to dress well as this made a better impression on people. Sometimes we would meet my ma and granny in the Kylemore if they were up town doing a bit of shopping. Then we'd head home to get ready for our next day of selling. There was a lot to organise and we were always our own bosses. You had to get the wrapping paper and set it together in lots of five sheets. It was a lot of work but worth every penny of it. Selling in town was hard work especially in the freezing cold and, oh, my God, the cold really got to you at times. I used to run off on Anita and sneak in for a cup of tea. She would go mad sometimes but I would just laugh at her. But I was always very proud of Anita. She was very clever and like me always thinking of ways to make a few bob. Even before we were old enough to sell on Henry Street we went down to the markets and bought about eight or ten trays of peaches. We had a dolly with us, a two-wheeler cart to carry boxes on, so we put all the peaches on the dolly and went on the DART to Baldoyle to sell them around the doors. The peaches fell all over the DART but we rescued them all and sold them anyway. We didn't go around the doors in town because nearly all the dealers from Henry Street were from town and they would have their own stuff.

12

But there were sad times too . . .

Because my da drank so much my ma at times just wasn't able to deal with it. She just had enough and even though she had five kids she would pack all our belongings into black plastic bags and off on the boat she would take us to England. She didn't want us to live that life. We were like yo-yos but she didn't care. She was a very strong woman and only wanted the best for us and that didn't include drink. The first time she took us to England she brought us to her auntie's house. The second time she took us to stay with her sister-in-law. I remember one other time when we ended up in this beautiful hostel. Funnily enough, I have fond memories of that hostel because when you walked in the front door it was just so warm and welcoming. The whole hostel was spotless; you wouldn't see a speck of dirt. I was very happy there and I remember we always had my ma beside us and she made us feel safe in the world wherever we were. She always had money when she travelled because my granny would give it to her. Within a couple of days of arriving at the hostel we started school. I hated every minute of school because I just couldn't settle in and then we had to do P.E in our underwear. Well I was so embarrassed; I just couldn't understand why they would run around in a gym in their underwear. I suppose I was very modest and to this day I still am. It would always be only a couple of weeks before my da would find us and beg my ma to come back home again. You know his promises: "*I'm sorry, Martha. I'll never drink again.*" She would always give in to him and we would be back home again.

Growing up, I never held this against my da. I know how much we meant to him because if he didn't love us he would never have followed but he always did.

However, when I was eleven years old my ma and da broke up. I was devastated and took it very badly. My ma and da meant everything to me. But I could do nothing about it and my ma moved to Baldoyle which at the time was like moving to the country. She wanted to get away from the drugs that were starting to really take their toll on the lives of those living in the inner city. During this time I lived with Mary and Skinner for about a year. I blamed my ma for the break-up as I guess I thought it was her fault. I remember every night in bed I would pray to God, '*Please, God, please, God, bring my ma and da back together again.*' I never stopped praying. In September of that year, just twelve years old I started secondary school in Kings Inn Street School. I went to school on the first day with no books and not even a school bag. My ma would have been the first to buy them for me, but I wouldn't tell her because I didn't want to worry her as she was away from my da. But anyway getting back to that first day in secondary school, the teacher came into the class and stood me up in front of the whole class and asked me where my books were. *"I haven't got any,"* I told her.

"Why?" she said.

"Because my ma is going to buy them tomorrow."

I felt really embarrassed by this and that was the last day I spent in that school. I was too scared to go back. I ended up going to school in Parnell Square instead. This school was okay but I knew I would have done better at Kings Inn. A lot of the kids at Parnell got into trouble and I guess never gave the teachers a chance. I have to say the teachers were very good though. I used to feel sorry for the quiet kids because they always got bullied. I used to say to them, *"Don't allow them to bully you. Stand up to them."* I hated bullies.

Anita came to Parnell Square for a year to do a work experience course. I remember saying to Anita, *"Don't do that. Stay at Kings Inn and do your exams. because you are smart."* Anita was clever and she worked hard. Sometimes we would be down in the yard messing and playing about and Anita would be at home studying. I remember she got a 'B' in her History test and I tell you none of our friends ever did this well so I thought Anita was just brilliant. And I know if my ma and da hadn't broken up I would have done as well. But I was proud of Anita and I told her that she could be anything she wanted to be. Anita would just say to me, *"Jenna Cahill, you think you know it all and you don't."*

"Well, Anita," I would say, *"I know you can do better."*

* * *

The year of the big snowstorm in Ireland was a great year for me. I was living with Mary and Skinner in the city when my da came into visit me and asked me to go home with him. He lived in Fairview. I was always really close to my da especially when he and my ma broke up. I guess he confided in me a lot. So off we went down towards Fairview with the snow pelting down.

I turned to my da and said, *"Da, why don't you come home to Baldoyle?"*

"No, Jenna, your ma won't let me in," he answered.

"Da, she will, because she always says that she wouldn't throw a dog out in that weather so I know she will allow you to come in."

This particular night the roads were bare and white. It was beautiful all around. My da and I walked and hitched and ended up walking for a long time. Finally we hitched a lift all the way to Baldoyle. When my ma opened the door I said to her, *"Ma, will you allow my da to come back home?"*

"Jenna, only if you all come back home and go to school out here," she replied

"Okay, Ma. We will. I promise." I was really happy about this because we were a family again.

Soon after that I started school at St Mary's Secondary School in Baldoyle. I remember my first day at school there. I was made to feel really welcome by all the girls and the teachers. I loved that school from the first day I arrived and I knew I was going to do well. I must say that all the girls were very good in class and really wanted to learn. They paid attention to the teachers. I could see the difference between school in Baldoyle and in the city. I suppose the parents were more involved with their kids and really wanted them to learn. In the city I know that we were brought up thinking that education wasn't important. It was who you knew that got you places. But my ma always said that education was important and wherever you went it went along with you. So I knew that I was going to try my best there and achieve all that I could. I planned to sit my Inter Cert. there the first year. This was difficult for me as I was three years behind but I knew I had to do it so I worked very hard day and night. After school most days the teachers would give me private tuition in Maths and English. I took all the help I could and studied very hard. However, the teachers thought that this was too much for me and wanted me to take a break so they gave me a week off school to go back to see my friends in the inner city. They also thought that I should go back a year and re-sit the Group Cert. I agreed to this, but when I got into the other class I didn't like it. I guess I missed the girls from my old class. In the end the teachers put me where I was going to be happy. I worked hard, sat my Inter Cert. and passed it. I was delighted and so were the teachers. I then decided to go on and do my Leaving Certificate but I hated every minute of this year. The reason I hated fifth year was that for nearly every subject the classes changed and I wasn't good with change. Instead I went to Leinster College in Rathmines to do a secretarial course. I sat the Pitman exam and passed with distinction. I was proud of myself but I had pushed myself all the way. When I finished in Leinster College, I made my decision to move away from Ireland.

* * *

I met Paul, my future husband, when I was about nine years old. Paul grew up in Dominick Street Flats and I grew up a few minutes away in St. Joseph's Mansions. All Paul's friends hung around with my friends. Anytime we would have discos down our way, we always invited them and any time there was discos around their way we always went to them. I really liked Paul because he always had great respect for girls. When I was twelve Paul was my boyfriend. This lasted three whole nights. When I moved to Baldoyle I didn't see Paul for four years and then one Sunday afternoon I went to a disco in Parnell Square, and met him again. When the slow set started, Paul asked me up to dance. He walked me home to my aunt's house down in Sean MacDermott Street, in the Gloucester Diamond. I will always remember that night. We talked about moving away. I said I was going to go to America and he said that he was going to Yorkshire to his cousins. I knew that one day I was going to marry this fella. We just hit it off from the beginning. I knew he had a bit of sense and this was hard to find in someone around our way so we became best friends and started to see each other a lot. I was doing the secretarial course over in Leinster College in Rathmines at the time and Paul was working as a welder. He took me to the pictures one night a week and then another night we went for a drink. I remember one particular night when Paul took me to the pictures and he bought me a packet of emerald sweets and a can of Club Orange. I was afraid to eat the sweets in front of him so I saved them until I went home to Anita's house. I actually couldn't wait to see Anita because I wanted to show her the sweets and share them with her. I was so excited.

Anita and I had a feast on the top bunk bed and I told her all about that first night out with Paul. After a while I felt bad because Paul was spending all his money on me, so I decided that Paul and I should work together on Saturdays. I went around Baldoyle and asked people if they wanted their grass cut and their windows cleaned. I got a good bit of work for myself and Paul. The money we made we kept for going out over the weekend. Paul would come down to my aunt's house to collect me and we would get the Dart out to Baldoyle where my ma and da lived. We had a lot of good times out there. There was always a gang of us out there every night. It was harmless fun, eating toasted cheese sandwiches, drinking pots of tea and having a lot of laughs. As the summer approached, I used to suggest to Paul that we go out and cut grass and clean windows to make a few bob together. I would have the day's work lined up for both of us and every Saturday morning Paul would come out and we would get to work.

My next plan was that we should try selling in Henry Street. We started selling stockings that we got through the wholesalers in Phibsborough. We also sold to all the houses in Baldoyle and O'Devaney Gardens near where my ma lived. The demand was great and we were doing so well that we also started selling underwear, pajamas, and track suits. I tell you we were well away and made a lot of money. The most important thing to me was always to make a profit, no matter how small it was. I always had loads of money but to be honest I never thought of putting it in the bank. People didn't use banks, at least street traders didn't. I kept my money up in my bedroom and in my pocket. My brothers and sisters would be looking for a loan so they always asked because they knew I had loads. I used to say to them, *"Jesus, no problem and you don't even have to pay me back, because I don't spend it on anything."*

But I knew that money was important in life if you wanted to make a good life for your family. Around this time I did a woodwork course in Sean MacDermott Street at Rutland Street School. It was just brilliant and the laughs were great. My cousin Tracey, Anita's sister, did the course with me and she was just the funniest girl. She just made us all laugh. I remember one day all the lads were saying she was fat, and I said to her, *"Tracey don't mind them. You're not fat. The only place you are fat is your belly."* Later it turned out that she was pregnant. Well at least I was honest with her. We were there to learn, but I don't think Tracey was. She used to put her Walkman in her ears, switch on the music and when you would try to talk to her she would just scream, *"What? What?"* She was just stone mad. But it was a good time in our lives.

Soon after this Paul and I moved to London. God, we only lasted there for about two weeks and then we headed to Jersey Island.

* * *

In the late 80s, Fr Paul Lavelle, parish priest of Sean MacDermott Street, tried to introduce boys and girls from privileged backgrounds to my world and the world of hundreds of families like mine living in the inner city in what was known as a deprived area. Eighteen-year-old school-leavers from exclusive schools would live for forty-eight hours in deprived areas in Dublin. Local people would invite them into their homes, presbyteries and social centres. The only requirement for taking part in this 'urban plunge' was a sleeping bag. The aim of the programme was to bring about an awareness of the problems of injustice, poverty and social conditions in Dublin's deprived areas. During the forty-eight hours the 'plungers' visited day centres for the elderly, youth projects, co-ops, Dublin courts and listened to talks from young people and met politicians, Gardai and the bishop of the area. I suppose they were trying to build a bridge between cultures. We had no idea how they lived and they had no idea how we lived and both sides were suspicious of each other. We didn't have half the material things that these kids had but what we could show them was a sense of community that was unique to our area and absent from the more affluent areas of Dublin at that time.

One day I was in my Aunt Mary's, Anita's ma's house, when a neighbour of hers, Jerry O' Callaghan, came by and asked if Anita, Margaret and I would like to go on the radio to talk about where we lived and what we thought of people who lived on the outskirts of Dublin City in places like Foxrock and Blackrock. The radio programme was Marian Finucane's *Liveline* and the show was to be part of the Urban Plunge, and there was to be a sort of 'blind date' between a girl and a boy from the different areas. Jesus, we were so excited we all said, *"Yes."* A journalist, Colm Keane, from the Marian Finucane Show came to Anita's ma's house to interview us. We represented the inner city. He asked us a lot of questions like what we thought of the people from Foxrock. They asked us to give our point of view and I said, *"It doesn't matter where you live; it's how you live that matters."* Three boys from St Conleth's, Belvedere College and Gonzaga schools were also interviewed. Colm just asked what their lives were like and their opinion of people in the inner city. The next week they picked one from each team to go on a blind date and I was picked. The night of the blind date the fella from Foxrock came to pick me up at my aunt's house with a bunch of roses and a box of Black Magic Chocolates. I was with Paul at the time but he didn't mind at all and waited there until I came back. I got to choose where to go so I chose Funderland at the R.D.S. and then to go to McDonald's later. He was very surprised by this because he thought that I would want to go to a pub, because I was from the inner city. We had a really good time together and the next day we went back on the show and talked about how we got on.

The fella was asked would he like to go out with me on a date and he said, *"Yes."* All I remember saying was that I was happy with my boyfriend and wanted to stay with him. But I was asked what my ambitions were in life and I said that one day I would like to go to America to live and maybe one day build my own house. It was only when I started writing this book that I thought about that day and how my life turned out. And I often wondered down through the years how that young man from St Conleth's school, Sean Pittock, had turned out. Did he fulfil his dream to become a doctor? At times it would even come up in conversation around the table when we were having our cups of tea and people would often say, *"Jenna, did you ever hear anything about that man and how his life went? Wouldn't it be great to know what he is doing with his life today? I wonder did he ever become a doctor. I wonder did he ever get married. Has he got children?"*

So that was it, I had to find out. I knew it wasn't going to be an easy task and maybe not even possible because I didn't even know his surname. But I knew his first name was Sean and with the help of Fr Lavelle and Liam Byrne who were part of the Urban Plunge I discovered that he did indeed achieve his dream and that he now worked in the Mayo Clinic, one of the finest hospitals in the world. I eventually made contact and the moment I heard the Dublin voice on the line I knew it was Sean. I was a little nervous because I didn't know how he was going to react but just like all of those years ago he was very friendly and had very fond memories of the 'urban plunge' and our 'blind date'.

Through our conversation I learnt that he had gone to school at St Conleth's and then had gone on to study medicine at UCD. And most amazingly I learnt that he had been working in America in Boston City Hospital in 1994 the same year that I had Jonathan in Boston. Sean's life has turned out very well and I am happy for him. Just before he left for Boston he met his wife, Siobhan, in a bar across the road from St James Hospital in Dublin while he was doing his training there. Siobhan is a paediatric endocrinologist. Recently I went to meet Sean's mother and sister in Killiney and we had a wonderful afternoon looking at photos of the Urban Plunge date and, of course, having several cups of tea.

Liam Byrne, one of the organisers, still works with the kids in the inner city and puts a lot of the success that the kids are having today down to services such as the

Lourdes Youth Service which was set up in the city in the 80s. He said that back then with little education and the young kids leaving school after only fifth and sixth class often there was nowhere for them to go. The Lourdes Youth Service created jobs. This year it celebrates twenty-one years in action. The children can attend the service from around the age of sixteen until twenty-five. A lot of kids who have gone through have come out with a trade and maintain jobs. Some actually went on to start up their own business and are very successful today. As the years went on, the L.Y.S created even more opportunities as the needs arose, providing social skills, literacy skills and computer training. Most of the children like me who grew up in the 70s, and later had children of their own, wanted different futures for their children. We know the importance of education and make sure our children stay in school, finish full-time secondary school and go on to college. But in some areas there is still room for improvement. The Irish Financial Services Centre, on the doorstep of these deprived areas, works together with Fás and Larkin College to create jobs for these young kids who may be at risk of dropping out of the system. They have to do Fás courses at night-time to get their skills and then after secondary school some go to work at the Irish Financial Services Centre where they are trained as secretaries or accountants. They really have to be committed and some are.

* * *

Living in Baldoyle was a lot like living in the inner city or maybe we were just lucky with where we lived and the neighbours we had. But my ma is the sort of woman that would get on anywhere as she is so liked and helpful to people. She re-created in Baldoyle the kind of community spirit that existed in the flats. One of our neighbours who lived next door to us in Baldoyle was one such neighbour that we became very close to. Mary's husband was in America and she worked as a nurse's aid in Portmarnock. One particular night Anita and I were babysitting for her and when we babysat we stayed overnight because she had two young kids. We were delighted to get a few bob and also to have the house to ourselves. Paul was with us that night but had to leave to get the last bus into town. One of the children had a rare form of autistic spectrum disorder so we had to be very careful especially when we were going to bed. We had to make sure that the kitchen and sitting-room doors were locked with a key and that we put the key on top of the kitchen door so that the little one would not be able to reach it. We were lying in bed one night when I turned to Anita and said, *"Anita, I can smell smoke."*

"Yes, Jenna. I can smell it too."

So with that we both got up out of bed to find the house full of smoke. But we couldn't see any fire. However what caused the smoke was the fire that had been left from the night before. The little boy had thrown a plastic boxing bag into the fire and it was smouldering away all night giving off smoke. My ma and da were just next door but we didn't go in and tell them. I don't know why. That night we all ended up sleeping in the sitting room with the windows open. When next morning Mary arrived home she didn't know what to expect when she saw all her belongings out in the front garden. She thought that we were all dead.

I swear it was some lesson that we learnt that night. We could have been killed because we did not realise that smoke is the one thing that can kill ye first. That morning we went into my ma and told her what happened.

"Jenna, if anything ever happens like that again, don't be afraid to come in and tell me."

Over the next few days we were just sitting around talking about it and thanking God that everything was okay, but my ma and da were too nervous to allow us to do it again. Soon after that Mary went to America after her husband and that was about fourteen years ago and to this day I still keep in touch with her. Even though moving from the inner city was a big wrench for me, I made good friends out there and forged strong bonds such as we had done in the inner city with our old gang. My ma had a lot to do with this as she is held in great respect by everyone. She is so wise and everyone comes to her for an opinion and she is never wrong. I met Caroline when I was fourteen years old. My sister Miriam got to know Caroline before me. But then she headed off to England and Caroline still came down to our house for a cup of tea and this is how we became friends. When Caroline met Yano, who later became her husband, she wanted my ma's opinion on Yano so she brought him down to our house and my ma said that he was grand but quiet. This was good enough for Caroline and she married him. They are still together today. We had great laughs in Baldoyle and even though Miriam, Sharon and I shared a room we still made room for Caroline to stay over with us. It must have been strange for Caroline because the first to bed in our house got to pick the bed that they wanted to sleep in and the first up next morning got to wear the best underwear, because we all shared our underwear and socks, I often laughed at this because Caroline never had that problem. She had a big house with even her own bathroom, never mind her own underwear. This would never have been heard of in our house. But I have to say we had bathrooms in our house in Baldoyle and I swear we thought we were millionaires.

I tell you I was no angel growing up and even when I hung around with Caroline I was up to devilment. One day, Caroline and I decided to run away. We were just looking for attention, as usual. I was working in Londis at the time and Caroline was working in Peter Marks in Grafton Street. We planned that I would go into her job and we would take off from there. We were just going to go to Wexford, and only for a weekend just to see if our families would miss us. So off I went into Peter Marks with toilet rolls and tea bags and a few other things to save us money when we got there. Caroline finished work and on our way to the train station we both decided that we wouldn't do it. We got the train home and got off at Bayside and walked by my house and then headed up to Caroline's. I remember going in Caroline's back door through her bedroom and up the stairs to her ma. We told Susie what we were planning to do and I swear she just started to cry. I felt sorry for her because we thought it was a big joke and our mothers were very upset. But that running-away episode was not a success.

* * *

Caroline's mother had a big garage so Caroline and I decided to use this space to teach the local kids dancing. Every Sunday afternoon we would hold dancing classes. We didn't charge them for their lessons but we just asked for money for refreshments. We never made any money for ourselves. I brought my love of music and dance all the way out to Baldoyle with me. Just like in the flats I was always organising things for the kids to do. One particular day I arranged with a friend of my da's who had a mini van, to drive a bunch of kids to Mosney, back to Butlins. He agreed and I paid him for the journey. Yano and Maureen, Caroline's sister, came with us but Caroline and I were in charge. Now all my family was in Butlins at the time and Caroline and Maureen were having such a good time that they didn't want to leave. I couldn't stay because it was my responsibility to get those kids home safely. I really didn't mind. When I got home I went out that night with Paul so I was happy.

* * *

On Fathers' Day in 1983 our world fell apart. My ma and da had gone out for a few drinks. My da went to meet his friends in Parnell Square and my ma went to another pub in Summerhill to meet her friends. This was the way all the couples in the flats socialised. They would go out together and came home together but they went their separate ways in between. At the end of the night my da always came to collect my ma and they would get a taxi home together. This night my cousin and I were out in Baldoyle wondering where my ma and da had got to. I wondered what was keeping my ma and da as they were usually home by a certain time. I thought to myself, *"Ah they're off having a good time; maybe they went to a party."* But as the night wore on and on I started to get more and more worried. Finally we couldn't stay awake any longer and we went to bed. The next morning we woke up and ma and da were still not home. Jesus, at this stage I was really scared and worried. Then the phone rang. It was my ma. *"Jenna, your da is in hospital."*

I rushed to the Richmond Hospital, to see my da. It was worse than I expected. I walked in and there he was all bandaged up. All I remember was that he looked like a mummy. I was very upset and worse was to come when we were told that he had to have brain surgery. Oh, my God, this was serious and the doctors didn't know if he was going to make it or not.

I remember going over and talking to him but he didn't even know who I was so I had to tell him. *"Da,"* I said, "It's Jenna." He couldn't respond and this really hurt me. He was in hospital for a long time and his life hung in the balance. The first operation relieved some of the pressure on his brain but he had to have another operation soon after that. The doctors had hoped that the first operation would be enough but it wasn't. It was a horrific time for the whole family. We loved our da and we just wanted him home. He was eventually discharged from hospital but he still faced a long battle ahead. He had to re-learn everything such was the damage to his brain.

He didn't know how to walk or even say a sentence, and he still didn't recognise any of us. But we all took turns and helped him. My ma was very tough on him as she felt she had to be cruel to be kind. She encouraged him to do things for himself even though it was hard for her to watch him struggle, but I tell you after a few weeks he was beginning to learn again. I remember sitting in the sitting-room with him and teaching him how to say sentences. It was very hard to see my da going through this, but finally with a lot of help he did get better. One of the things that he did for a long time after was to pick up in his hand a piece of hot coal that had fallen from the fire. Sometimes you would cry just to watch him but sometimes we laughed at some of the mistakes he would make. I think the stress and anxiety would get to you and all you could do was laugh.

When he was out of danger my ma was able to tell us what had happened that fateful night. When my da had gone to collect my ma they could see an argument starting up in the pub so my da had said to my ma, *"Martha, I'm going out to get a taxi."* He went outside to get the taxi and he found a young girl lying on the ground. He had gone over to pick her up when he got a smack on the head with an iron bar. He was just in the wrong place at the wrong time but I was very proud of him and how he had gone to save this girl's life. I still thank God that he got better. My da is very brave as this had been the second time that he had put his own life in danger trying to save another person's life.

13

When I was sixteen I went to America for the first time in my life. Caroline and I went over to stay with her aunt. The morning that we were going I just couldn't believe that I was actually going to America, the place I had always dreamed of, and where I had told everyone on the radio I had plans for. Caroline's ma came down to my house and picked me up and we all headed for Dublin Airport. We were so excited that the flight seemed to be over in moments. And then touchdown in Boston, the place I always dreamed of, America. My eyes were opened wide. What I saw just fascinated me . . . the highways, the trucks, the heat. Oh, God, the heat! It must have been 90 degrees in the shade that day. I remember so well coming in from the airport. We were sitting on the back of a truck singing Neil Diamond's 'We're coming to America'. It was such a good feeling. I knew even then that this was going to be my future home, that I would one day live here.

Caroline's Aunt Sarah was so good to us and she made us very welcome so I had a nice introduction to the country so many Irish people had to flee to in order to get work. Sarah brought us everywhere including Cape Cod where she had a summer house right beside Hyannis beach where the famous Kennedy family took their holidays. I tell you I was just fascinated by the whole lot. We were spoiled rotten. She brought us to all the best shops and gave us spending money to buy presents for everybody back home. She also brought us to a restaurant where I had my first experience of the American phenomenon of 'all you can eat' piled up high on your plate. Now this was unbelievable because back then there was none of this in Ireland. What I remember most about that restaurant was the chocolate pudding. Oh, that was just gorgeous and I don't know how many of them I ate. The whole holiday was brilliant as everything was so different from back in Ireland. We also headed off on a very long bus journey to Virginia where Caroline's other aunt lived. She brought us to an enormous fun park where my eyes were just out on sticks with all that was new to me. Everything was larger than life; even the ice creams were huge. Well, you know yourselves, when you got an ice-cream off the corner man in Ireland two licks and it was gone. But not in America! You wouldn't be able to finish the thing. She also gave us one hundred dollars each to spend, which was a huge amount of money back then. It was like winning the Lotto. Sure you wouldn't get that for a week's wages in Ireland as things were so bad with the economy and unemployment in the 1980s. I felt so lucky to be seeing such great places at just sixteen years of age. Back in Boston, Caroline's sister Maureen worked in a big house with a swimming pool and she was allowed to bring us to visit that house. Even the train stations in America were fascinating and so different. We spent three weeks in America and then we returned to Ireland. I have to say we had a wonderful holiday and after that is it any wonder that I knew you could have a good life and earn good money in America?

While I loved my trip to America I never liked the summers that much as a teenager. I guess I just didn't like sitting out in the sun. I remember one year all my family went to Spain for a holiday when we lived in Baldoyle. My ma had a ticket for me but I didn't want to go. I was allowed to stay home as long as Anita stayed with me. Of course, Anita and I had thought this was just great fun altogether, the whole house to ourselves. But instead of throwing a party the first thing we did was get in and clean the whole house from top to bottom. We were like two old housewives. Honestly I don't know what it was with me and cleaning but I was just fascinated with it. It was probably the way my ma reared us. She would always say, *"Cleanliness is next to godliness"* and I think that kept me interested in everywhere being clean.

During our week of playing house Anita's ma, Mary, came out on the back of her son Kevin's motor bike to see if we were okay because we still didn't have a telephone. Now that was something that didn't normally happen so Anita and I thought this was great fun. Well, we actually thought that Mary was stone mad. Now I can't remember if she even had a helmet on her. But I do know that she was wearing a skirt because Mary never wore trousers.

Anyway we sat out in the back garden that afternoon and entertained Mary and Kevin with cups of tea and a chat. At the end of those two weeks that my ma was away, she arrived home to two apple cakes with welcome home written on the top of them. We were so excited and proud of ourselves that we had survived. My ma was exhausted when she came back but she was very happy about those cakes and, of course, to see that the place was shining.

When I wasn't playing house and cleaning and scrubbing, I always tried to get a summer job to earn a few bob for my future life in America. My favourite job was on the vegetable counter in Londis in Bayside. Of course, being the saleswoman I was and having the hard experience of selling on Henry Street, this job was no bother to me. I always had the customers around me. If I wasn't there or maybe had a day off they would always come into the shop and ask where I was. Coming up to closing time and you would have to get rid of the vegetables before they went off, so I would seel them off at a cheaper price. I would give good deals and I was never left with old fruit or vegetables that had to be thrown out or wasted. The fun that we had in that shop was great with the customers and the staff. To this day I keep in touch with some of the girls that I worked with. I had experiences in Baldoyle that I would not have had if we had stayed in the city. The culture was so different to what I had known and even though we were only a few miles from St Joseph's Mansions we were in another world. Going to a 'debs dance' for the first time was a big thing for me as I was the first out of all our cousins to go to one. So, I had to be beautiful. My granny didn't have a clue what a 'debs' was and was puzzled by the whole idea. I suppose in the inner city at that time we didn't stay in school long enough to need to go to one. But my ma rose to the occasion as usual and got a beautiful dress made for me by her cousin's wife's sister who lived in Blanchardstown. My ma knew exactly what would look good on me. She had good taste so I left it up to her. So between her and the dressmaker I had a beautiful dress. All the kids that I had taught to dance came to our garden to see me dressed up. They always looked up to me and Caroline. I guess we were like role models to them. When Caroline came down to our house I thought she looked stunning and she did. Of course, there had to be a party in our house to see us off on our big adventure and it continued on through the night even after we left.

* * *

When I went to America with Paul to live, I was homesick for the first six years. My first days there with Paul were exciting but heartbreaking; I felt that I had left my family forever, and that there was no going back. Being from a big family with a lot of laughter this was hard to let go of. We stayed with Caroline and Yano for a weekend and then found our own apartment. The night we moved into our apartment I remember Paul and I going down to David's Square and sitting down on the benches. Here I just lay in Paul's arms and cried, thinking of my family that I had left behind. I don't know how I stuck it out but I did. I remember I used to send letters home to my family and later on I found out that they used to cry and hand the letter around to each other and they would be all in the kitchen sobbing their eyes out. I laughed when they told me this because I didn't realise that my letters were so sad. But I was speaking from the heart.

I remember going to Irish pubs where they played Irish music all the time. This just touched my heart and a lot of other Irish people's also. It was funny because if there was Irish music playing in Dublin you wouldn't even want to listen to it. Now I have to say this doesn't happen to everyone and certainly does not happen to me because I just love Irish music altogether, but, when you are away from home everything is different. And, of course, when you are away from home, no matter where you are, on the street, in a pub or just on a bus and you meet another Irish person you just take to them straightaway. Wherever you are in the world the Irish really look out for each other and sometimes you just feel like you are part of one big family. All you would hear in the Irish pubs was, *"What part of Ireland are you from?"* And straightaway it would lead into a conversation.

But the happiness didn't last long and I suppose looking back I should have seen the warning signs a lot earlier. When I was just eighteen years old, Paul and I broke up for a short period of time. I came home from America and to cheer myself up I went with some cousins and friends to Blackpool on a holiday. The laugh was just ninety. We would be in our hotel room and some of the girls would be doing shows and stripping off. They were just hilarious and we never stopped laughing on that holiday. One of the other girls and I decided to stay in

Blackpool and we got a job in one of the cabaret bars. There we were behind the bar serving all the drinks out. All our friends would come up to the bar to us thinking we would give them free drink, but they came to the wrong person when they came to me because I didn't give out one drink for free. I would be afraid I would get caught and never thought that it was worth it. But it was our first night working there and our last. We decided that we were going home but we missed our flight home and went to Liverpool to stay with friends. I nearly died when we arrived at the flat. It was filthy and there were four of us sleeping in a single bed. I would have been much happier sleeping in the airport. The lady that we stayed with though was really nice to us and her daughters brought us to a dance. But it was a rave and the smell of hash nearly knocked us out. So the next day our mothers had to pay to get us home. When we got home my brother said that I had to ring Paul. Of course, I rang and he asked me to meet him on O'Connell Street that night. I did meet him and we both fell into each other's arms. I have to say it was a good feeling. I had met another guy and I felt sorry for him but, he understood. Paul and I soon returned to America and Paul asked me to marry him. I will always remember how Paul proposed. My sister Diane and her husband Neill had married and came to America to visit us for their honeymoon. They were thinking of staying, and they had come to see what they thought of it. The day they arrived Paul and I went to pick them up at the airport and as a surprise for them we had a limousine waiting outside. I remember Diane saying, *"Oh, look at that limousine"* and I said to her, *"That's for you.*" She couldn't believe it. That was a good moment. It was our wedding present to them and I was just so happy to have them there. Always thinking of business and doing well the next day I had job interviews set up for Diane and a painting job for Neill. I think they thought I was mad. There they were coming to me for their honeymoon and I had them ready for work. They were cursing me down to the ground. For the weekend, we all decided to go to Martha's Vineyard in Cape Cod. Cape Cod is where all the rich and beautiful have holiday homes. We had a great holiday and on our way home from there Paul proposed to me. We were in the car and Diane and Neill were asleep. Paul just said to me, "*I think it's time we tied the knot.*" All I remember saying to him was, "*Ask me again in two weeks.*" I said this because when we broke up a few years earlier the most important thing to me was that we were together and that we had each other. Marriage didn't mean that much to me then. And, yes, two weeks to the very day Paul asked me again. And this time the answer was yes. We saved very hard for that whole year and together we saved eighteen thousand dollars in that short period of time. Now we worked very hard to make that kind of money.

* * *

Paul and I became husband and wife on 11th October 1991. When we arrived at Dublin Airport the morning we came home from America to get married, both our families were there to meet us. This was a wonderful day for us and a day that I will never forget. It had been two years since we were last home, so seeing everyone was fantastic. There were people at our wedding that we hadn't seen in years so it was a good way to see everyone at one time. On the morning of our wedding Miriam and I were in the bedroom and Miriam happened to look out the window. The next thing, she shouted out, *"Jenna, Jenna, look at your horse and carriage."* It was gorgeous and, oh, my God, I felt like the Queen. We were all jumping up and down with excitement. I was twenty-three but that morning I felt like a little child. I was so excited. There was a lot of commotion in our house that morning. The flower girls were getting the rags out of their hair and they were crying their eyes out. They were being tortured but they had to put up with all the grown-ups telling them to shut up because they had to look beautiful. All the neighbours were coming in one after the other and the house was packed that morning. There were about three different people doing my make-up but I didn't care as long as it was being done. And the video man was going around interviewing everyone. He was even pushing the bathroom door in on people for the laugh. Everyone was just mad. One moment someone's shoes were lost – the next moment it was someone's dress. The commotion never stopped. And, of course, the singsongs down in the kitchen were endless. As I walked down the stairs everyone in the hall was shouting, crying and whooping with delight and happiness for me. Out to my carriage I went. The carriage had two white horses with flowers running up their reins and red velvet on the interior of the coach. It was magical. And, of course, no Dublin wedding would be complete without a 'grushie'. This is when the family of the person getting married would throw money to all the kids in the neighbourhood and they would be out early lined up waiting for it. I had five bridesmaids and five groomsmen, two flower girls and two pageboys. Our bridesmaids wore purple dresses, and our groomsmen were in black. The groomsmen and bridesmaids on the wedding cake were the same colour. I was, of course, in white while Paul wore a white jacket and purple bow and sash around his waist. The little girls were in white dresses with purple ribbons while the little boys were dressed the same as Paul. So mine was a big wedding. We had about two hundred people at the meal that day. I walked down that aisle with my head held high and I felt very proud. My da was so proud of me but it was hard for him to let go. While I loved the church ceremony, some of the guests couldn't wait for it to be over so that they could start the celebrations. We went to Saint Anne's Park for our photographs to be taken against the beautiful flowers of the rose garden. After the photographs we went on to the reception and this moment was really special for me. Seeing everyone there, just for me, filled my heart with joy and my eyes with tears. Even the cake was more beautiful than I could have imagined three layers high with a waterfall underneath it. I found it hard to believe that all of this was for me. The meal was followed by the speeches. Oh, my da, he was gas but heart filling when he gave his speech. When he said, *"I'm losing a good daughter,"* I replied, *"Da, you will always have me."* He really is an old softie and we are very close. Then the music started and everyone got up to dance. And, of course, I always loved dancing so I had to go around everyone for a dance. By the end of the night everyone was crying as we started saying our goodbyes. I didn't't know why because Paul and I had been living in America for a while at this stage. Before we left Paul took off my garter and threw it out to the girls. Then everyone made a bridge and we ran through it hugging and kissing everyone. It seemed to go on forever, as did the tears. After the wedding reception that day Paul and I stayed in a hotel in Howth for our wedding night while the party went on all through the night at home. We went over to Blackpool for our honeymoon the next day and then headed down to Yorkshire to Paul's aunt and uncle where we had a great time, though I never really wanted to go on a honeymoon as I hadn't seen my family for two years and I would have been quite happy to stay around.

With the honeymoon over, it was back to America and to work. I worked for the same family in America for eight and a half years. I liked my job and the family was really good to me but it was hard work too. In the winter they would light the fire some days and then when I was cleaning the fire out the next morning I swear I felt like Cinderella. I really hoped that one day I would not have to clean out fires or clean houses ever again. Now I know there's no harm in doing that kind of work but I just had had enough of it after grafting for years in the cold in Ireland and then coming to America cleaning, waitressing and cleaning out fires. I had had enough and I just wanted to do something else with my life. I often thought of going to college, and hopefully one day I will have enough money to go to college. I really don't know what I want to study yet but this is my next dream. I feel it's important to have a dream or a goal in life because it gives you something to look forward to and makes life more interesting. I always have to have a dream or goal to work towards. America did so much for me and for the many who emigrated there in the 70s and 80s. But even when you have settled in America you never forget where you come from and it's always lovely to go back to Ireland for a visit.

I remember one year Paul and I came home for Christmas like many other Irish people. I didn't have a Green Card, so I was illegal in America. Going back and forth to America was nerve-wracking as I always worried about not getting back. And to be honest I often had to lie to immigration. I had to say I was working in Ireland and only going to America on holidays. My cousin who had his own business pretended I worked as a secretary for him. The day before I went back to America I went down to his office in Ballybough and made sure I had my story straight because I had a funny feeling that I was going to be stopped and sure enough I was right. They stopped me and brought me into a room and interviewed me. They rang my cousin's secretary and asked her loads of questions. Luckily I had gone down to her the day before because we both had our story right. Eventually they allowed me to board the plane and, boy, I was relieved. This was a big problem for all the illegal Irish in America as most people were afraid to take the chance of coming home. Later when they started giving out Green Cards to all Irish people we had to send forms in with all our information on it. This then went into what they call a lottery and if you were lucky your name got picked. The reason behind this was, of course, to make people pay their taxes. The American economy needed the taxes of so many illegal immigrants doing well in good jobs. Everyone I knew got their Green Card and then after paying taxes for five years you could go forward and apply for citizenship and an American passport. This made visiting home and living in America a lot easier.

*   *   *

Our happiness was complete, (or so I thought) when I gave birth to our son Jonathan on the 2nd of May 1994. This was the year of the World Cup and an exciting year for all the Irish. It was a Sunday afternoon in Boston and I felt a bit strange, so I went to the doctor. I was checked to see if I was in labour but I wasn't so they sent me home. However, that evening, Paul and Paul's two sisters and I were sitting watching television and I felt something was wrong. I never said anything to them, because I wasn't sure if it was going to be a false alarm again. So off I went into the bedroom and called my friend Caroline. *"Caroline, I think I might be in labour."*

"Jenna, how often are the pains coming?"

"Jesus, Caroline, they're coming every five minutes."

"Jenna, you're in labour. I'm coming right down. Don't worry. You'll be all right."

In the meantime I called the doctor but as she was telling me what to do the pains were getting so bad that I had to get down on the floor. Between pains I would start to laugh but I guess this was because I was so nervous because, I'm telling you, labour pains are no laugh. But there, standing in the middle of the sitting room, were Paul and his two sisters laughing as well. I guess we were all laughing with our nerves. But then the pain would come back again and I would say to them, *"Oh, don't laugh now because the pain is coming back"* and off I started screaming and crying again.

Caroline arrived soon after with her sister Maureen, so at this stage I had an audience. Paul drove me to the hospital and Caroline came with me. All through the journey I remember pulling Caroline's hair and saying, *"Caroline, please make the pain go away."* But that pain was going to stay with me for a while, whether I liked it or not, and it continued to get worse. At the hospital one of the nurses rubbed my head and told me to imagine I was on a wave. How was I to imagine I was on waves with this pain? Pam, the midwife, came to my rescue. She was from Dublin and a friend of Caroline's but I think that made it worse. I really wanted to curse like mad but I was afraid because Pam was from Ireland and I thought she would get mad at me. So I had to be very good and just scream. Now not only was Pam there from Dublin but Paul's sister was there along with Caroline and Maureen, and, of course, Paul. I was in so much pain I couldn't tell them to get out. But, still I was really embarrassed. There was me naked with all them looking at me. Now looking back I can laugh at it but not at the time.

I remember saying to Pam, *"Oh Pam, please help me. Give me an epidural. Just get the pain away."* Then I heard Maureen saying, *"She will have that baby by ten past two"* So even though I was in a lot of pain I was watching that clock. She was right. At nine minutes past two o'clock I gave birth to an 8lb 7oz baby boy. I was so happy. I tell you becoming a mother was just the best day of my life. There was nothing like having that baby in my arms. I thought that all my friends should have a baby because it was great. The hospital was like a hotel and, on my last night there, the nurses took Jonathan so that Paul and I could have dinner in our room together. You could say it was our last meal together. From now on we were a family. There were three of us now so we would be busy. Now the day we had to take Jonathan home was a day in itself. I swear we were driving up one-way streets we were so nervous. We didn't want anything to happen to our new little baby. We finally made it home safe and sound. My ma and da came over from Ireland for five weeks and this was great because even though I took care of kids for a living, it's definitely different when it is your own child. I suppose you feel so protective. I went back to work a week after I had Jonathan. I don't know how I did it. Work wasn't important anymore, all I wanted was to stay home with my baby. But Paul felt we needed the money and I should go back to work. So that was it.

I suppose I knew no better but I think I probably went back to work too soon. It wasn't good for me or Jonathan as I was working about fifty hours a week at this stage. I breast-fed Jonathan but when my ma saw all my time taken up, she suggested I get a breast pump so that she could feed Jonathan in the middle of the night. Now using that breast pump was very funny. We had what's called a pantry in our house in America; I guess it wasn't much smaller than our scullery in the flats. This is where I went to do all my pumping, so if anyone was looking for me I would shout, *"Moo, moo . . . I'm in here."* I guess I felt like a cow at times.

My job wasn't too bad as I just took care of two children and a house for two doctors. But at times it was bad. The pressure of working and being a mother was hard. I had to take Jonathan to work with me. I had no choice. Working mothers have it hard and even today it is no different. You feel guilty all of the time even though you know you have to make money to have a good life and to give your child all he or she needs. Sometimes I would feel terrible taking Jonathan out on those cold winter days. And one time when I was taking the two girls I was minding to piano lessons I had to take Jonathan along with me. My ma had made Jonathan's bottles for that day and when I went to feed him every bottle had spilt all over the bag. I had to run back home and make new bottles. Jonathan was only about four weeks old but my ma told me to put Jonathan on powdered milk as well as breast milk to give myself a break.

I put myself under a lot of pressure to do everything perfectly, to be a good mother and a good worker, and I was finding it hard.

I continued to work for another four years, but as Jonathan was getting older and more demanding I did fewer hours. But I liked my job and the people were very good to me. We were living in the Somerville area of Boston for about seven years at this stage and I really loved our apartment. However, one day the landlord told us that he needed the apartment for his daughter. We were a little sad as now we had to find somewhere else to live. I rang a good friend of ours for whom we had done some work over the years. He had a big house in Cambridge just across the road from my job. The house was empty because he was trying to sell it and when I told him our story he let us move into the house. He was a decent guy and he even insisted on buying us new carpets for the bedrooms. I was very happy and I suppose hard work paid off in the end. The only thing I found hard was living and working on the same street.

14

One day when Jonathan was about three I said to Rhonda, the daughter of my ma's best friend who had been living with us for two years and was almost like a sister to me, *"Rhonda, I think there's something wrong with Paul."*

"Jenna, he is all right."

"No, Rhonda, there's definitely something wrong."

I didn't put too much thought into it over the next few weeks but on the Fourth of July, Independence Day, our friend gave a big party and we were all invited. I didn't go because I thought there was definitely something wrong. I was worried and annoyed at the same time. Paul brought Jonathan to the party and never asked me if I wanted to go. When he came home that afternoon, he told me that Rhonda would have to leave or he was leaving. I tell you I was shocked at this but very sad as well to have to tell my friend to leave. He had really hurt my feelings and I did not want my friend to leave. Over that weekend my ma and my sisters and Rhonda were mad at me and I didn't blame them. I wasn't able to stand up to Paul. This is when things started to go badly wrong with my life. I started to feel depressed all the time and I didn't understand what was happening. I knew that I was sad. All the music and laughter had been taken away. Thinking back, I would say I probably had a nervous breakdown. But I thought that maybe telling Rhonda to leave would make things a bit better between myself and Paul. When Rhonda left, I continued to work and take Jonathan to work with me. The loss of a friend and the thoughts of Paul wanting to leave never left me. When I was at work and Jonathan was asleep or maybe with Paul, everything would get too much for me to handle. I remember one time being in my employer's kitchen and crying on my knees to my boss for help. I guess he felt sorry for me but was not sure what he could do. He would talk to me and try and make me feel good. But sometimes when I was in the job on my own I would go up to their bedroom and fall on the ground and be wrapped up in a ball crying and trying to understand why Paul would do such a thing when I didn't know what I had done wrong. I was in a foreign country with all my family back in Ireland and no one to turn to. I was lost for the love of family and friends. With waiting for the purchase of land to come through in Ireland, this didn't help my situation at all. I always felt there was no future ahead and that life was letting me down badly

The husband and wife I worked for in America were top doctors who were very high up in their specialist fields. They also travelled a lot and depended on me and I never let them down. When I started with them their two girls were only two and half and five years old. They were very easy to take care of and I became very close to them quite quickly. I brought into that job all I had as a child, including a love of acting, singing and dancing. Through the most crucial years of their lives I gave them the best I could by doing what came naturally to me. I worked about sixty to seventy hours a week sometimes. Their house was big and open plan and very inviting and warm. Some Saturday nights I worked also and if I was going out afterwards to the Irish pubs I would get ready there. The girls liked to see me dress up and when my bosses came in they always said I looked good. They saw a different side to me then. Each day I would teach them something whether it was a song or a little bit of acting. I would always have them looking nice and do their hair every day. And in the evening while they were having their bath I would say to them, *"Think of a word, any word, and I will sing a song to that word."* They would do it and, of course, I would always have a song and they would just laugh at me. These girls loved to read and this is something I learned from them because for me growing up, the importance or love of reading wasn't instilled into us. And when I had my son I always read to him from the moment he was born. Because their parents travelled so much I spent a lot of time with the children. When the day they were due home came, I would get the girls to bake something special for them and make a banner with 'Welcome home' on it. We would hang it outside their front door and this made their return home special and the girls would be so proud of themselves. So when I left work every day I always felt happy and was always proud of the job I had done.

At home things did not improve between Paul and me and I still could not forgive him for sending Rhonda home. Paul wasn't great at giving me compliments. He would just say that when I didn't look well he would tell me. Thinking back now this wasn't good enough because every woman needs a compliment now and again. Over the years this was part of the reason I lost my confidence. Every year I just got deeper and deeper into that depression. I would like to get this message across to men especially if their wives or girlfriends are suffering with postnatal depression, or any kind of depression. Depression is caused by a chemical imbalance in your body and you are helpless to stop it when it starts. But I did not recognise it or understand how I got to this point. I liked Rhonda living with us. We really got along well and she was a great help with Jonathan. I was working full-time and being a mother and trying to keep your own house going as well as working full-time is really hard. Every night when I came home from work, Paul would be out at karate. So Rhonda, Jonathan and I would have a great time. We would be dancing and singing every night and the laughter was non-stop. I think this got to Paul at times so before he came in we would stop the music. This went on and on for a long time and life was just brilliant or at least I thought it was. I was the happiest mother in the world and I thought Paul was happy too. I actually wanted more kids straightaway but Paul wasn't ready so we waited. But time went on and on and I have to say I was upset that I didn't have another baby around those years when Jonathan was a baby. But then as time went on and Jonathan was getting older I was leaving the baby stage so having another baby didn't bother me as much. I was still very happy and I had no idea what was ahead of me.

* * *

I was about twenty-seven years of age when depression first hit me. I didn't know what was happening to me but I knew something inside me was changing and I didn't like it. I went for some counselling, and after a few weeks of that, I thought I was okay. But you know I wasn't. So it was nearly a year before I thought to get help again. I wasn't totally sad all the time. Sometimes I was happy and sometimes I tried very hard to be happy, well, at least when I was around people. I didn't want anyone to know what I was going through because I was embarrassed about it. I think depression is an illness that people don't go around talking about. I was a very happy girl, always singing and dancing and that just all went away. I was really mad because Jonathan had a mother who had been happy and I wanted Jonathan to have that happy mother back again. But that mother was really mad at herself and started to, well, I guess I could use the word, neglect herself.

I wouldn't go shopping for clothes any more. I felt I didn't deserve them because I wasn't that happy person. I kept seeking help but never got any better. I know my depression was hard for Paul to deal with and he didn't know what to do to help me. He just kept saying to me, *"Jenna, get help."* I really was trying and nothing seemed to work. I worked for a psychiatrist in America and she recommended that I take medication. I told my ma about this but, she kept saying, *"Jenna, don't go on medication. You don't need it"*. I listened to my ma and never took anything but to be honest if it was now I would listen to the psychiatrist. It was too bad I didn't because I suffered for a very long time, suffering that I really didn't have to go through at all.

This went on and on for years. For a very long time Paul and I were trying to buy a house in Ireland as this is where we thought we were going to live eventually. Even though we were living in America we figured it would be a great investment. We would rent the house out so that way it would be paying for itself. One day I was in Ireland for a holiday with Jonathan. I heard from one of Paul's family that there was land for sale in Balrothery in north County Dublin. I thought about it and decided to have a look at it. I knew where Balbriggan was but not Balrothery, so off I went to see the land. I have to say on the drive out I fell in love with it: the fabulous view, the fields, the cows, the horses. It was like going to the country and yet only a half hour from the city centre. I absolutely loved the area and thought it would be a great place to bring a child up. I was overjoyed and rang that night and told her I was very interested. Now the vendor wanted twenty-two thousand pounds for a third of an acre. That was a lot of money back then But it felt like the right place and we could at last build our own house. It was another dream about to come true. We bought the land but it took about two years for everything to go through. It actually took two years. There were times when we felt like giving up but eventually we were ready to find a builder. There was another site next to ours and the people who had bought that site built their house first. We had a look around their house and it was absolutely gorgeous. I talked to their builder and gave him the job to build ours. We told him that there was no hurry and he could build it in his own time. This suited both of us. It took the best part of a year to build but it was the only thing I could feel happiness about. This was indeed a dream come true for me and one that I had expressed all those years ago on Marian Finucane's *Liveline* radio show. We moved back to Ireland and sent a container of furniture home. We stayed in Ireland for a year, but Paul couldn't settle and wanted to return to America. I didn't mind because I just wanted him to be happy because he always tried to make me happy. I suppose maybe Paul was afraid of losing the great business we had built up. Shamrock Painting had a great reputation and we had worked hard to make it the financial success it was.

Paul returned to America ahead of me in May of 1998. A few months later I returned too I had just been waiting for Jonathan to finish the school year. I always worried about Jonathan finishing school because I knew school was very important for him. I guess this had something to do with the way my schooling had gone and as you see that hadn't gone too well. This was a good year for me. I decided that I would do my G.E.D which is a high school diploma in America, the equivalent of the Leaving

Certificate. Now I have to say I don't think it's half as hard as the Leaving Certificate. Anyway I passed the exam and got my diploma. This meant that I could at any stage go on to college. Maybe one day I'll do that but not right now.

The next couple of years weren't too bad. Paul and I did really well for ourselves financially but deep in my heart I still wanted to move back to Ireland. I was so confused about life and didn't know what was best for my son. A lot of Irish people move back home to Ireland when they have children because they want to be near their families and for their children to be educated in Ireland

That year we did a lot of travelling. We had worked hard and had earned a break so the following November on Thanksgiving we headed to the Caribbean island of Aruba for the holiday of a lifetime. We flew from Logan Airport in Boston and in just three hours it was hard to believe we were on one of the cleanest and the safest islands in the Caribbean. Though on the way to our hotel we saw a lot of poverty and that made me feel uncomfortable. Our hotel was beautiful and I swear the food was unbelievable. Ours was an all-inclusive holiday so once you were there all the food and drinks, even alcoholic, were included in the price. We got a room overlooking the ocean; this was a bit more expensive but I guess it was worth it, because when Paul and I were sitting on the porch at night we could still hear the music and watch the sunset. Now I know I sound romantic but I really mean it, the sunset and the sky at night were absolutely gorgeous. The holiday was like a dream come true. The food was laid out so you could just help yourself. You could also book the restaurant overlooking the ocean. I used to say to Paul, *"Paul, you sit down. I'll get your food for you. What would you like?"* I didn't mind helping Paul or Jonathan to anything they wanted because all I had to do was put it front of them. They even had an ice machine so you could help yourself at any time. When the buffet was over they served pizza and sandwiches at the bar 24 hours a day. I tell you, this was heaven.

We went on a few tours while we were there the most exciting of which was a safari. We rented our own Jeep and not only did we do a safari tour but we also saw a lot of the island. Aruba has the cleanest water in the world. I have to say you learn a lot about the world when you travel. I have a love of horses and on our trip to Aruba I decided to go riding with a group of people up into the mountains. I was excited about it but it turned out to be a disaster. My horse for sure had to be the one that was jumping all over the place. I was terrified and screaming, *"Mister, Mister, help me please!"* The man in charge told me to get off the horse and I tell you I never got back on. I was left in the middle of nowhere by myself and eventually a taxi came to pick me up. The most beautiful part of the island was the white, clean sand and the water which was as clear as day. You could see deep into the ocean. One day we went on a cruise and we all went scuba diving. It was magical and the boat ride was so relaxing. We were all very sad when the holiday came to an end and to this day Jonathan still says that it was the best holiday he ever had.

California was another great holiday for us. We did all the usual things like visiting Universal Studios and Disneyland, the first Disney ever built. We went on a tour of all the movie stars' houses and headed to Rodeo Drive where the movie *Pretty Woman* was made. I felt really good walking down this street. The only thing is you would want to have a small fortune with you to spend in those shops. Actually we were lucky to be able to get into the shops as most of them are by appointment only because this is where all the movie stars shop. During our trip to California we went to San Diego to Legoland. The whole fun park was made of Lego. While we were there we also visited the famous Hollywood Boulevard where all the stars' handprints are set in the pavement We had plenty of money at that time in our lives, more than we knew what to do with and we headed on to Florida to another Disney World

Florida is like a dream land. Everything about it, even the weather, is beautiful. We went to Alligator Land and Jonathan sat on a real alligator. We enjoyed those years of financial success and we made the most of it. We were all happy. After another two years in America and still doing really well, Paul and I decided to return to Ireland again. But after another year we returned to America. At this stage I didn't know what the hell was happening but I knew something was wrong and I really felt it. We were running from something. I was sick of moving apartments so we both decided to buy a house in America so that we would not have to move again. At this stage we were all sick of moving as it was having a bad effect on our lives.

Paul went off to America again ahead of Jonathan and me and bought a house. I saw pictures of the house on computer and liked it. Jonathan and I returned to America once again and sent all our furniture back too. What was happening to our lives? Something desperate was going on and we didn't know but we really were running. When we arrived in America and met Paul, there was tension straightaway. Paul was tense and so was I. We had an argument at the airport so straightaway there was tension. It just didn't feel right. I guess deep down I felt trapped and this was it. There was no going back to Ireland. I knew I had to stay in America, especially as we had now bought the house.

When I arrived at the house, I cried and told Paul that I didn't like the wallpaper or the kitchen. But it was nothing to do with the house. It was all the pressure and I felt Paul was distant. Over the next few months things didn't go well at all. I was very unhappy. Jonathan was very unhappy and Paul was unhappy. We thought Jonathan missed his friends in Ireland. I missed my friends, family and just the way of life back home. America didn't feel like home any more. The house and material things didn't matter at this stage. We were all very unhappy people. A few months later after a lot of thinking we decided that Jonathan and I would return to Ireland. Paul said that he loved us so much that he would do anything for us and that he would follow us home after he sold the house. The house was hard to sell as the war between America and Iraq had just started. This upset Paul.

Paul returned to Ireland for Christmas for three weeks

and we had a really good time. We were even trying to have a new baby.

He returned to Ireland again in February for another week.

The night before he was due to fly to America he casually said, *"I want you and Jonathan to come back to America with me now."* I swear I still didn't know that my marriage was about to break up. I said to Paul, *"Wait until Jonathan finishes school,"* because at this stage he had moved school twice and I didn't want him to be moved a third time. If I had known then what I know now, things might have being different. Just weeks later, that's when I received the worse phone call of my life on the 18th March.

15

When I went back to America in May things did not go well at all. Paul packed his bags and left the day that Jonathan and I arrived. I suggested he live in the basement apartment of our house but he moved out. He came back at first each day to take showers but just weeks later Paul stayed away from us for five months. One day Jonathan and I were driving down Massachusetts Avenue when we spotted Paul. He looked happy even though he hadn't seen Jonathan in quite a while. I was wondering to myself how he could go without seeing his own kid and be so happy. I just didn't understand this at all. I cried my eyes out. Afterwards I was bringing Jonathan to the shops and I was still crying some three hours later. When we stopped outside, Jonathan turned around to me and said, *"Mam, you just write your book and get it published."* That was the night that I decided to get stuck in and write the story of my life. I should mention here that when we were in

Ireland Jonathan joined Aer Lingus Swimming Club and while he was training I would chat to another mum, telling her stories about my childhood and where I grew up. One day she asked if I had ever thought of writing a book. I hadn't but when I became depressed I decided to give it a go and I found it really helped me.

That day on Massachusetts Avenue it was as if Jonathan was saying to me in his own way, *'Mam, don't mind him. We will be fine.'*

Soon after this Paul got himself a lawyer and told me that he wanted a divorce. I nearly died but what could I do? I could only agree and give him what he wanted. I figured that there's no sense in holding on to someone who doesn't want you. We had to sort out the property and money we shared. So Paul made an agreement which seemed pretty fair but didn't work out, so I decided that I should get my own lawyer. None of this seemed right to me but I guess it did to Paul. Well, the first thing my lawyer had to do was to put a stop to the house being sold in America.

"I don't want to do that; that house needs to be sold."

She would say to me, *"Stop it and let me do my job. I just need you to be in court."*

I nearly died. 'Court'. I didn't want to go to court. I thought we could come to an agreement outside court. The following Wednesday I had to turn up in court. I cried my eyes out. All I could think of was how you can be with someone for all those years and then it ends like this. I tell you I would rather have had nothing than to fight over money. We were going to court that day to deal with the custody of Jonathan. If I wanted to return to Ireland with Jonathan, I had to go through the court system. If I just left

America without a court order I could be brought back to America and even arrested. So I really had to listen. Deep down I didn't think Paul would keep anything on me but at the same time I did have to listen to the lawyer. We filed for the divorce. Paul would not accept the divorce papers and therefore never turned up in court. So that court date was a waste of time. It broke my heart that day because that was the first day I was ever in court in my life. Eventually Paul accepted the court papers and within a few days Paul and I had to face each other in court. This wasn't too bad though because we had come to an agreement the day before. I didn't care about anything other than that I could leave America with my child. Nothing else mattered at that time. When I arrived in court that day the first person I met was Paul. He couldn't look at me eye to eye but I said hello to him because I had no hatred in me. I didn't think it was a good idea to hold a grudge. In the courtroom Paul sat behind and I thought he looked very angry. I was still shocked even though it was months later. I went into that courtroom with my head held high and with a smile on my face because I knew that I would be able to return to Ireland with Jonathan, even though I was facing divorce.

The divorce doesn't really bother me any more because now I look to my future. Maybe one day I will meet someone who will love Jonathan and me. Paul met another girl and all I say to that now is good luck to both of them. Jonathan has to handle what happened between him and Paul in his own way. All I can do is be the best mother to Jonathan that I possibly can.

* * *

While I was in America I sought help from a therapist. I knew this particular doctor so I called her on the phone one night and told her my story, and she met me the following day. Then pretty much every day from then on I spoke with her. Over those months I learned a lot about depression and what I had been going through. I'm still learning a lot about myself in therapy and finding out more about my childhood. I have learned that when I was a baby I was very sick and spent a lot of time in a fever hospital. My parents were not allowed to see me, except through a glass window. My therapist reckons that my depression goes way back to that time. If a baby is parted from its mother for more than two weeks in the first two years of life, the child feels abandoned and that child is prone to depression later. I was one of those kids. I think this is also the reason why my mother's and father's separation was very hard for me to handle. I guess I don't fare well with separation. But time is a great healer and things do get better. One of the great joys of my life has been writing this book. It never felt like hard work. Cleaning houses is hard work; writing is not.

During those years moving back and forth between Ireland and America I was running to try to find happiness and find a way to get rid of the terrible sadness. It felt like being in a dark room for a long time When I was depressed, I couldn't so much as make a decision for myself. Month by month, week by week, day by day it just got worse, until one day I found myself at the lowest point in my life. I decided to allow everyone else to make my decisions for me and once they said I was doing the right thing then I believed them and it felt safe. But if I had to make the decision totally on my own I never felt safe. If Jonathan wanted to go to the shop then if Paul said it was OK I felt good about it. But, if Paul wasn't around and I had to make the decision for myself I would think that something was going to happen to him. I never felt safe until he was home. It was terrible. I really feel that I lost seven years of my life. I gained my confidence back little by little during that therapy. I'm not afraid now to make decisions for myself and Jonathan. I can honestly say that now I feel very confident about making decisions. However, now that I can make decisions, sometimes I feel people want to make them for me. I guess they were so used to me asking them over the years and now it's all new to them, that they feel I'm the same old Jenna. But, thank God, I'm not. I know people are only trying to help and I tell you people can be so good but now I have to depend on me!

Now that I look back, this break-up may have been the best thing for me. It woke me up to reality and snapped me out of my depression. Maybe if it hadn't happened I would be still in the same old rut. I was running to try to find happiness and find a way to get rid of the terrible sadness. I came out of it finally and I am determined never to look back. The only way now to look is to the future. I have to say here that if you feel you are depressed, get help straightaway and stay with it. It is just like any other sickness and it does go away. The hardest part of all is the effect our break-up had on our son, Jonathan. His heart was broken and his life was torn apart. We both had a lot of anger inside us that we had to let out. I cried mine out and a lot of the time I took it out on my ma and da. I didn't mean to do this but they understood. I guess we take our anger out on the people we feel safest with, and most of the time that's our parents. Jonathan suffered a lot through the loss of his father. It was hard but as I got help this also helped me to help Jonathan. I didn't always handle the situation well but then I learned to use better words and a different tone of voice and this helped a great deal. Day by day it got better. I guess because I feel safe and strong, Jonathan is also feeling safe in the world now. I know there are days when I feel down, but, those days I just have to make sure my feelings don't rub off on him. During these times Jonathan took to reading and read every day for about two hours. I rewarded him with a packet of magic cards and by doing this, it encouraged him to read more. So on the down-days he would turn to a book, which I thought was really good. Now that we are in Ireland the reading has been put on hold for a while. I guess he is having too much fun with his friends, so that is good. He loves Ireland but what kid doesn't? They have so much freedom. I think when a child goes through a break-up people need to be very considerate because he or she suffers no matter what. They have feelings just as we do. But the more stable their lives stay, the better for them, and the more people that stay constant in their lives the easier it is for the child to cope. I feel very sad for Jonathan as he loves his dad so much. They were best buddies, but kids are resilient and sometimes they can get through difficult situations more quickly than we as adults can. I know Jonathan is going to do well in his life because he is a very determined child and definitely has a lot of me in him. When I look back at my childhood and think about the time my ma and da broke up I went through difficult times, and got through them. My family played a huge part in my recovery and survival. They made sure they were there for me during the really hard times. I remember in June of 2003 when my brother Gerard and his girlfriend Celine were on their world tour. They decided to leave Australia because Jonathan and I were going through a rough time and they wanted to come to America and visit us. We were delighted to have them stay with us. They stayed for about six weeks and we made the most of that time. I brought them to New Hampshire to Cape Cod to the Irish Village, and, of course, to New York. I drove all the way from Boston to New York and we got there by 9.30 that morning. We hit all the sights, the Empire State Building, Ground Zero, the Statue of Liberty and Ellis Island. We headed for Central Park and across the road to the Plaza Hotel where the film *Home Alone* was made. I just wanted to show Jonathan the hotel because he loves the movie. He was delighted with himself but, with the cheapest room at four hundred dollars a night, for sure we weren't going to stay there.

We did all of the sights in one day between ten o'clock and five o clock, not bad at all. Looking back on that trip it meant so much to Jonathan and me at that difficult time. I was pleased and felt strong once more. Sometimes the only faces you want to see are those of your family. Gerard and I had great chats and I got to know my brother really well during that visit. I felt I got so close to him. He is just such a nice man. All he kept saying was, *"Don't worry, Jenna. We'll make it."*

Jonathan and I arrived home in Ireland for the final

time on the 25th November 2003. I felt such relief when I stepped off the plane because everything was sorted out and the pressure was off. All of my family helped us out and when I walked into my home I have to say I walked into a mansion. The house had been freshly painted by my da and brother and my ma, sisters and my ma's friend Jean helped unload the container of furniture. They emptied all the boxes and sorted out the house and it was just great to have it all done by the time we walked into the house. All I had to do was get my computer ready and start writing again. I have to say though I was very happy not to be around for the container arrival. I knew what they were all in for. It was hard work. With the support of friends and family we have survived. My family is a great support and constantly there for me. My ma couldn't do enough for me. She is just the best. I'm happy to have so many people who love me and Jonathan in my life. One day I hope I can be such great support to someone if they ever need me. Maybe one day I will come to understand the whole thing. And I hope that one day I can say Paul did me a favour. Because now when I look back I can see that Paul and I should have changed some things about our lives together.

On the thirteenth of December of that year my ma and da were forty years married and all the family celebrated it down in the local pub in Baldoyle. The place was bopping with young and old and it was the first time that I had been out since I had come back from America. Nothing about the way our family celebrated occasions had changed and I was happy about that. Everyone was standing up singing, dancing and holding hands. It was a good laugh with a four-course meal thrown in. I had salmon and my ma was surprised. *"Jenna, it's Christmas and you're getting salmon."*

You know my ma and da's generation. Unless you're eating turkey and ham, you're not having a Christmas dinner. After the meal all the ladies headed to the bathroom two at a time. It was like the old days but in a lovely way. *"Jesus, my hair is in bits,"* or *"I hate when it goes curly,"* *"I tell you, the years are creeping up on us. We're getting old."* I was standing in the queue when a woman comes running in singing and relating her story to another woman, *"I was here last night and met a man and you know what? He asked me to walk his bike home."* The woman beside me turned around and said, *"Jaysus the bleeding cheek of him asking you to walk a bike home and he not even asking to walk you home."*

The Dublin humour hadn't disappeared while I was in Boston. The party was supposed to be a surprise for my ma and da, but, when Jean, my ma's friend, came over to America to see me and my ma back in September, as soon as she got off the plane she told my ma, *"Martha we're all going down to Grainger's to celebrate your fortieth anniversary."* I have to say my ma was so excited that we were doing something nice for them. I tried to stop Jean but it was too late. I just stood there laughing.

That Christmas was my first Christmas without Paul in eighteen years. We got through it very well and Jonathan was just brilliant. He was a great help to me around the house and it was my first time to give Jonathan a job and wages every week. He cut the grass and helped make the beds. We also did a lot of fun things together like going ice-skating and other outings. It was a wonderful Christmas until one day after New Year Jonathan and I were in a shopping centre with my ma and my ma's kids when I happened to bump into a friend of mine from Boston. *"Jenna, how are you? Your ex-husband Paul was on the same flight as me coming home."*

I nearly died. He had come all the way to Ireland and didn't as much as visit Jonathan. Jonathan was there when the girl said this, so of course he was very hurt. Oh, my God I thought the hurt was over by now. All that day Jonathan continued to ask me, *"Mam, why did you not tell me? Why?"*

"Jonathan, I didn't know."

"Yes, you did, mam. Yes, you did. Mam, I wanted to see him."

"Jonathan, it's not my fault."

Well, that day was tough and Jonathan went to bed very sad that night. I know that Jonathan has gone through hell over this break-up but I also know that one day he will come out a much stronger kid and will never ever hurt his kids or wife. I know that day will come.

* * *

Just when I thought life was settling down for Jonathan and me a letter arrived in the post the following summer. It was from Paul's lawyer in America. I swear I just hated getting these letters. They got me down. There was another court date set for September. It was too short notice for me and I was not able to turn up. The judge was not happy but he made a decision that day even though I wasn't in court that our house in Ireland was to be sold and the proceeds split in half when Jonathan reached eighteen years of age. There was a lot said that really upset me and my lawyer who was in court that day phoned to tell me how the appearance had gone. That did it for me. I was so upset because if there was one thing that hurt me it was that I wanted more than anything else for Paul to see Jonathan. So this is when I felt the real fight burning in me. There was another court date set for the fifteen of November, so that was it. I was going to change lawyers. I engaged a new lawyer recommended to me by a friend. It cost fifteen thousand dollars – which I hadn't got but I felt it would be worth it and I was prepared to give it my best shot. I was wondering how I was going to prove that Paul was working and how much money he was making. It was said that he was not working and had very little money. That was not going to stop me. In fact it just made me determined to fight harder. I went down to the bank to get copies of all bank statements going right back to 1992. This was what I needed because it showed how much money we had been able to save. We had a month to get ready and it was very hard and tiring and emotionally upsetting for everyone. I managed to find some of the jobs Paul had done that summer and got the names and addresses for my lawyer. She subpoenaed these people along with paint stores to prove that he had bought paint at this time. Tax records showed for the last four years how much he had earned. With all this information I knew I was going into court with a fighting chance. We had built up a very successful business and I was going to prove to the court just how successful Shamrock Painting was. My ma was great throughout the whole case. She kept saying, *"Jenna, you will come out on top,"* and I believed in her because it's very seldom that she's wrong. So with all my information to hand I was ready for the next court date. I had confidence in my new lawyer and I knew I was going to do better. My ma and I headed off to Boston once again for another court date. I wasn't nervous this time. We landed in Boston on the 11th of November 2004 to stay with a friend in Somerville. The next morning I had to meet with my lawyer at 10 am. And later that day we were having a four-way meeting with Paul and his lawyer and me and my lawyer. I still wasn't nervous and was wondering why not. Paul and his lawyer went into the conference room. My lawyer gave Paul all the facts that we had gathered on paper hoping that we could come to a settlement outside court. But I knew this was not going to happen. Later my lawyer brought me into the room. I felt really good and full of confidence. When I saw Paul I did not feel that I wanted to be with him again. I swear. We couldn't come to any agreement so we knew that we would have to go to court. In the room I turned to Paul and said, *"You know, I know every job that you did so I will get all those names and addresses.*

No man was going to put me and my son out of our home. Paul wanted the house in Ireland to be sold and split in half. The only thing we sorted in that room that day was maintenance for Jonathan. I said that Paul could see Jonathan any time of the year he wanted. The only time that we would not be around was July as we were going on holiday. He could have Jonathan in America for three to four weeks during summer. Paul wanted Jonathan to spend Christmas with him. I said that he could take Jonathan on Christmas Eve from nine in the morning until five or six that evening and on Christmas Day from three o'clock. He could also take him to America until the eighth of January. I thought this was fair, but, Paul said that he would just take him next Christmas instead and would see him in February for four days. That was all that happened that day but I was happy to have that sorted for Jonathan's sake. Paul was a very good father to Jonathan when we were a family and I always wanted him to see his son as often as possible. The two of them get on great together and always have a good time. I talked to my lawyer later that day and she advised me to find as many jobs as I possibly could that Paul had done that summer to show the judge on Monday morning. We were going to have a lot of fun because at that minute I really didn't think that would be possible. My ma was waiting outside and she wasn't surprised that nothing had happened. She felt it was better that the case was to go in front of the judge. Once again she built my confidence up. The only thing I was worried about was going home and telling Jonathan that he wasn't going to spend Christmas with his dad. That was really on my mind. Of course, my ma said that I should allow Jonathan to spend Christmas with Paul. *"It's only one day, Jenna."*

"Ma, you're right. It's more important that the child is happy."

"Jenna, he can't suffer any more. He has suffered enough."

Over the next couple of days I had my work cut out for me. My friend loaned me her car and my ma and I went around getting names and addresses of the customers Paul had worked for over the past years and hopefully over the summer of 2004. So Saturday morning at the crack of dawn and with the streets full of snow we set off. Our first stop was at a house in Cambridge where Paul had done a job two years ago. Now I knew where this and many other jobs were because I used to bring Paul a cup of tea to wherever he was working when we were together. We pulled up outside the door and I knocked while my ma waited in the car. Two little boys answered.

"Is your mother or father home?"

Their father came to the door.

"Hi, my name is Jenna. My husband painted your house a couple of years ago, Paul from Shamrock Painting Co."

"Oh, yes,"

So I told him that and Paul and I were going through a divorce and that Paul was claiming that he doesn't make any money. *"We are up in court on Monday morning and to be honest I only have one chance to fight this and to give it my best shot. Could you help me?"*

He invited me in and told me that it was his father who had hired Paul and that he was sure that he would help in every way he could. Once again I told the father the story. In their apartment they had cameras everywhere. They were so helpful. His wife gave me copies of the cheques that she had given to Paul and a copy of the invoice. This was just brilliant for me. I was in there at this stage for nearly an hour. Next the door bell rang. I looked at the television screen and you could see who was at the door.

It was my ma. I couldn't stop laughing. She was trying to look in through the glass door. From the inside we could see her but she couldn't see us. I said to the man, *"Ah it's just me ma. She came with me."* I went to open the door. *"Jaysus, Jenna, thank God you're still alive!"* I couldn't stop laughing. She thought that I had been murdered because I was taking so long. I guess she watches too much television. Back she went out to the car and after about fifteen minutes the doorbell rang again. It was my ma again and she needed to use the bathroom. I introduced her to the family and they were very nice and allowed my ma to use the bathroom. So we were chatting for a while and then we said our goodbye and they wished me well in court. Back we went into the car.

"Ma, were you worried?"

"Jenna, I thought you were being murdered and I didn't know where I was or where we were staying. Jenna, don't stay that long again."

I just couldn't stop laughing. She was so funny. When I looked at what I had in my hand I began to feel less nervous about going into court. All that day we went from house to house. We arrived at another job and there was no answer so I went to the neighbour's house and he told me the man's name. I already had his address. If I could just get a copy of the invoice it would be brilliant. We would come back there later in the evening. We had been working hard so we went for something to eat. I dropped my ma off for a while to shop while I knocked at a few more jobs. Off I went once again, door to door, getting names and address and trying to get as many invoices and copies of cheques as I possibly could. I went back down to the house in Cambridge to see if the people were home yet. There was a car in the driveway. I rang the doorbell time after time with no answer. I thought to myself there's no way I'm leaving here that easy because I know there is someone home With that a man came to the door in his boxer shorts with his dog beside him.

"Hi, my name is Jenna. My husband, Paul, from Shamrock Painting Co painted your house this summer. Could I talk to you for a minute?"

"Well, I was just napping and I'm not dressed."

"Well, would you like to get dressed? I don't mind waiting."

"Okay just give me a few minutes."

"All right, take as much time as you need."

To be honest I didn't care if he came to the door naked. But, I wasn't expecting to get very far with the man because he didn't know me from Adam. He came back to the door dressed this time and off I went with my speech.

"Hi, do you mind if I talk to you? It will just take a few minutes. I am going through a divorce and I would like it very much if you could give me a letter or a copy of the invoice just to show that Shamrock Painting Co. painted your house. I need to fight for my home. I have a little boy and if I don't prove this we could be made to sell our home and this is something I don't want to have to do. I know it's hard for you because you know Paul and not me and Paul did a good job on your house but, just do what you can."

"I need time to think about this," he told me.

"OK, thanks a million."

"Call back tomorrow."

"Okay."

Later on that evening we were still searching for information. Our next stop was another house that he had painted two years before. I knew this lady and knew that she would help me in every way that she could. Once again I knocked at the door. I explained to her what was happening and she told me to come in. She wrote me a beautiful letter stating that Paul had painted her house. She also told me about another house that Paul had painted. When I saw the house I was delighted because this was a big job. Brilliant! I reckoned it was about an eighteen-thousand-dollar job. The lady told me to call back to her house as she knew about other jobs he had done around Cambridge.

Once again the doorbell rang. The lady looked out at the side window of the front door. I told her my tale and she brought me into the hall. She couldn't give me a copy of the invoice but she would give me her name and address. While I was standing there I got the feeling that she wasn't giving me the right information. In the hall was a shelf with letters that had been mailed to her address so I did get the name and I memorised it. So this was all I needed. The most important thing that you need when you have to subpoena people is their names and addresses; otherwise the document is not valid. But it was strange because before I told this lady that Paul and I were going through a divorce she told me that Paul had painted two houses for her. I thought this was great because now I had four houses that he had painted this summer alone. Well, I had caught him out. At this stage it was about nine o' clock at night and we had to go back to the lady who had told us that she could show us all the houses. She was able to show me on a map the names of the streets that the houses he had painted were on. I already had these houses on my list but nevertheless I was very thankful to her. She wished me well. My ma and I called it a day at that stage as we were very tired. But remember we still had Sunday. So that night we went out for dinner and I swear I was nearly falling asleep in the restaurant. I just couldn't stay awake. But my poor ma was up talking and smoking half of the night.

So next morning we were up at the crack of dawn again out searching for more information. People were so good to us. I think that when people know that you are fighting for your home for your child they are very sympathetic. But I was glad that was the end of that. Monday morning and our court date arrived. I swear up until Sunday night I wasn't a bit nervous. But, come Sunday night I was so nervous and worried. I think it just got to me at that stage. But by Monday morning I was okay again. We got a taxi to the court but it turned out that my lawyer had got the wrong information and that we should have been out in Concord which was about forty minutes away. My lawyer arrived and gave us a lift. We had to wait to be called and I was anxious because Paul and his lawyer looked very happy indeed. I turned to my ma who just reassured me as usual and once again I began to feel positive.

Our lawyers went into a room with the judge first and then Paul and I were called in. I walked in with confidence; I was not a bit scared. The judge said that we had both worked very hard and done very well for ourselves. He told

Paul that he had a good business and he advised us not to go to trial with this. He recommended that I should get more maintenance and more that half of the value of the house. He sent us outside to try and solve it with our lawyers. And that is what we did. The settlement seemed fair as we didn't have to worry about losing our house and Jonathan is guaranteed his home to grow up in. Now that it's all over, I can see light at the end of the tunnel. I have a lot more good days than bad ones and I wake up every morning and go to bed every night, well, nearly every night, happy and feeling happiness inside that I hadn't felt in years.

*　　*　　*

Every night since the break-up I talk to God. I am not a very religious girl but when you go through bad times in your life you have to believe in someone and that someone for me was God. So, I would lie there in bed with my two arms under my head and say, *"Hello, God, it's me Jenna. God I'm asking you very deeply would you please bring me and Paul back together? I really want us to be a family again. Please, God, do your best."*

Now that was at the beginning of the break-up of my marriage. A few months into that I started to say to God, *"Hello, God. It's me, Jenna, again. God, I think you don't want us to be together. I know you will do your best. But, please just give me and Jonathan the strength to carry on with our lives."* Night after night this went on for months. I swear it wasn't easy but chatting to God made it a little bit easier for me. I guess I had someone to believe in. After a few months I started to say to God again, *"Hello, God. It's Jenna here again; God I think you don't want us to be together again. Well, God it's looking that way, and I'm beginning to understand. But, God, if I can ask you one more thing, will you bring Jonathan's daddy back to him. He didn't have to lose his daddy just because we broke up."* So I will continue to talk to God at night and maybe one day Jonathan and Paul will be best buddies again. That will mean more to me than anything else in the world. Those chats remind me of when I was a child and my ma and da broke up. There I was again asking God to bring my ma and da back together again. I know Paul and I won't be husband and wife again. God has chosen a different path for me and now I can live with that. When I look back at my life and even though I know it wasn't too bad there was a lot of struggle. I struggled to get a good education as I always wanted to do well. As for my childhood I think I had a great one and I was a child who was well loved by everybody. Yes, of course, there are some things that I would have liked to change but that's something that I can't do. I do hope that I can live my life now to the fullest and maybe one day I will meet someone who will believe in me and maybe I can share the rest of my life with him. I feel the strength that I had as a child, and lost through my depression, has come back to me now. I guess I really forgot how strong I actually was. I think if it wasn't for the break-up I would probably never have written this book and would probably still be depressed. Now I will continue to be strong and I have learnt how to become the person I want to be in life. There was one very good point that my counsellor made to me and that is that you are only responsible for your own behaviour. This made me do a lot of thinking. And, when you think of it, you can't be responsible for anyone else's behaviour.

16

Before I could feel that I had finished telling my story there were two places I felt compelled to visit to bring my story full circle. When my life fell apart I drew on the strengths of my childhood years and the people and the community that shaped me. One of those places had to be school. Rutland Street School played a big part in the lives of the north inner city community and it still does. Even though I didn't agree with how one of my teachers behaved when I was there, the kids now are lucky to have a dedicated and caring bunch. It was good to go back and see them and also to get a bit of information about what happens in that school today. Now it wasn't my first time back since I left; I went back about eight years ago. But this time, it was different and my life was very different. I asked Anita, my cousin, to ring the head teacher, Mrs. Adams, to ask if it was okay to visit. When I went to Rutland Street School she was known as Miss Tobin. I remember her well and I was very happy to hear that she was now head teacher. She just had a special way about her. Mrs. Adams became a member of the staff in Rutland Street School straight from college back in 1971 and in 1987 she became Principal. Anita was supposed to come with Anne (who is editing my book) and me but at the last minute she had to cancel.

When we arrived outside the school it looked pretty run-down but once we went through the front door we were greeted with a smile that made us feel so welcome. So what the building looked like on the outside was immaterial and, as the saying goes, it's what's inside that is important. And for sure the love and happiness that were there was just brilliant. Mrs. Adams, of course, being the head teacher, was busy on the phone but stopped to say, *"Go into the canteen and have yourself a cup of tea or coffee and I'll be with you in a minute."*

The ladies in the canteen were so cheerful and chatty and, of course, made us tea. Now I have to say even though they were full of chat and cheer they still worked very hard. We had our tea and chatted to the ladies while waiting for Mrs. Adams. Of course, the canteen was new to the school but, we were amazed at the food the children were being served. The ladies were peeling the potatoes from scratch, fresh every day. We were asking lots of questions and it was no problem for the ladies to give us the answers with pride and pleasure. What emanated from them was that they were very pleased and happy about their jobs. At 8.30 every morning breakfast begins for whatever child wants to go to school early.

School starts at 8.45. Breakfast consists of any cereal

they want from Rice Krispies, porridge and Coco Pops to fresh fruit, which gets delivered daily. The kids don't have to bring in a lunch because at twelve o'clock they get a hot dinner served to them, and it varies from day to day. From corned beef, potatoes and a fresh vegetable to chicken curry and rice another day. After dinner they can have fresh fruit again, yoghurt, or cheese. The meat is delivered fresh three times a week and while we were there the meat delivery arrived and the chicken to my surprise was the best of prepared fillets, only the best for these kids. And the good part is that the parents don't have to pay for it. Anne and I went into the dining room where the children's art is on display. It was brilliant and we were amazed at the standard of hand-writing from the fourth-class kids. I tell you there was a lot of talent to be seen. Mrs. Adams was very happy to see us and showed us around the school and we got to meet some of the teachers and visit the classrooms just for a few minutes. I tell you there was always one kid hanging out of Mrs. Adams getting hugs. I thought there was a lot of love shown. It was like she was a mother to all of these kids and brought out the best in them. For instance one child came in without his uniform and Mrs. Adams asked, *"Where is your uniform?"*

"Ah, it was in the washing machine. I was lucky to find this jumper, Miss."

"Well, will you have it tomorrow?"

"Yes, miss."

The kids showed great respect to Mrs. Adams and all of the teachers. Later, while we were in the lunch room, a kid came in looking for a football but when he saw us in there he said, *"Excuse me, Mrs Adams, I'm sorry for bothering you but is there a football in here?"*

Mrs Adams just replied with, *"Now haven't you very good manners. I'm so proud of you."* She cops onto and acknowledges all the good things that they do. When we went into one of the younger kids' class there was a little boy standing with his teacher busy in conversation. He must have been six. Mrs. Adams told us that he had been lucky enough to go on a trip to Disney World and she said to him, *"Tell these ladies what you told me."*

"I saw Mickey Mouse and he is real."

Mrs Adams said now she knows that Mickey Mouse is real because that little boy told her. I just turned to him and said, "I was there too and he is real." But from the lunch room to the classrooms all of the kids that we met had their confidence boosted by that wonderful teacher. She stopped another child and turned to us. *"You see this young lad? Do you know that he is student of the year this year? Tell them why."*

He was a bit shy so Mrs. Adams told us that this year he stays in class and doesn't mess. I thought this was a really marvellous way to reward him and to encourage him to stay in education. I have to say she is very proud of her students and the school. When we went to visit one of the other classrooms the teacher there, a Mrs. Daly, was actually my high babies' teacher and I remembered her well and likewise she remembered me, and my parents. One of the other teachers had taught my brother James and she remembered him too well. Mrs. Adams remembered Miriam but, you know what, it really shows you that these teachers love their jobs and where they work considering that they are all still there thirty years later. It says a lot about them and the love that they have for the people from the inner city. I couldn't believe the ratio that was in the classes. From high babies to second class there are only ten to fifteen kids in each class. After that around twenty-five kids in a class up to sixth class. There are one hundred pupils altogether with three full-time and one part-time assistant teacher, one reading teacher, one behaviour teacher, and one support teacher. The school even has a computer room and a computer in every classroom. I wondered if the school still put on plays because when we were there the school plays were big productions. Now they put on plays every Christmas and Bertie Ahern comes to watch every year. Even the President came to visit Rutland Street School.

The overall goal of the school is for the kids at least to go on to secondary school and hopefully to college. Mrs. Adams operated the S.C.P., the School Completion programme, in Rutland Street. There is an after-school homework programme and once a week the pupils visit the secondary school that they plan to attend, which is Larkin College down by the Diamond. They do homework there and also get to work with the Librarian. By doing this it gets the kids used to going in and out of that building so by the time they finish primary school they will be somewhat adjusted. Mrs. Adams also keeps track of the kids in first year in secondary school and sees how well they are doing.

* * *

And talking of keeping track of people it can be hard to

keep track of my big family. One thing I will say is that we are all still close and have a great love for one another. We have never fallen out with one another or lost contact with each other even though we have all gone on to lead very different lives. I think the glue that binds us is my ma and da and the love and affection they have for all of their kids and grandkids and nephews and nieces and their sense of what is important in life, people. I think all those years ago that we in the inner city taught the kids from privileged backgrounds that family, friends and neighbours are what carry you through life.

So, Davy, the eldest has three kids now. He is not married and he lives between England and Ireland and when he is in Ireland he stays with my ma and da in Baldoyle. When he comes home his kids come to see him all the time. He has spent most of his life away from home so I never really got to see him that much but he is a lovely person and it is always a pleasure to see him home.

Diane is married with three children: Nikita, Natalie, and Roslyn. Nikita is in college studying music and drama; Natalie and Roslyn are in secondary school. Diane is still a great friend to my ma and looks out for us all. My son Jonathan adores Diane and her girls.

James left school early after being spotted by an English football club. He was a very talented player and was in line to do very well. But he met the love of his life, Natasha, and when they had kids he missed his family too much and decided to leave. James is a very devoted father to his four children. His son, Clayton, plays soccer for Ireland's under-12's team and has gone abroad on trips to play for Ireland. He has definitely inherited his dad's skills. I don't see James as much as I would like to as he lives over one side of Dublin and I live over the other but we get together and catch up on all our news when we meet up at my ma's house.

Gerard has just finished travelling the world with his girlfriend Celine and they have just had a beautiful baby girl, Yasmin. They are over the moon.

Miriam is beautiful and always makes us laugh and smile. When we were younger we always wanted Miriam to come downstairs out of her bed in the mornings because she could make anyone smile. She lives with my ma and da and drives a taxi

And finally Gavin. Gavin did his Leaving Certificate and has plans to be an electrician. He is a great kid and a great help to my ma. He has done a few Fás courses and hopes to get a trade. He still wants to be an electrician and is just biding his time until the opportunity arises.

As for Anita's family, well, Skinner still lives in Gloucester Diamond in the inner city but Mary passed away on 11th September 2001, the day the Twin Towers were struck, and thousands of people were killed.

Anita and Gaza have three children and had always lived in town, but finally Anita moved to a beautiful house in Raheny. I never thought I would see the day that Anita would move out of town but she still goes back in nearly every day to see Skinner and to bring her kids into school. She also works in town helping out at a hostel for homeless people. I guess she surprised us all. I'm very happy for her and she loves her house and Gaza adores her. Anita and Gaza got married only last October and the wedding was a real Dublin affair. Sticking to tradition she chose to get married from her da Skinner's, house. He was the proudest man and he had no problem leaving his room for the wedding of his daughter. Anita and I are still very close and I get waited on hand and foot and Gaza won't even allow me to go near the kettle when I visit. He is a good man and a real family man. But as the saying goes behind every good man there's a good woman. But the inner city is still home to Anita's sister, Tracey. She loves it and I don't think she would ever move. She has three children but she is still mad and always loves to gossip but in a very nice way. She still makes me laugh when I see her. Margaret, Anita's other sister, also lives in town and has one child. My ma's house is still like a train station, always full of people, but that is the way she loves it. She is a friend to everyone and always has time and space for one more if they arrive along. She makes a huge dinner every day for whoever turns up and I love the fact that I can go there any day and she will put up a plate of dinner in front of Jonathan and me. She really is our inspiration. My granny who is eighty-four also still lives in town and wouldn't live anywhere else. She cooks a big dinner everyday and gives some to her neighbours because she says, *"Sure, God help them, they are too old to cook for themselves so I send over a bit of hot dinner to them."*

As for life growing up in the inner city maybe we didn't have a good education and maybe we had to fight hard for a lot of things, but one thing we never had to fight for was the love, care, honesty and friendship we had growing up in the inner city. We had parents and people that gave us their hearts and who had total commitment to us. I will never forget all the people who came into my life to help me become the person I am today. I am off all medication and I have finished with counselling. Jonathan is doing extremely well. He enjoys training with the Aer Lingus Swimming Team and has been accepted into one of the top secondary schools in Dublin. Like me he has great determination in life and strives always to do well. I am very proud of him.

Epilogue

It was the night of the St Patrick's Festival Sky-fest in 2004 and people from all over Dublin had come into the city to watch. I rang my ma and asked her if she would like to go over to visit my brother James in Crumlin. I collected her and we headed for the city centre. It was bumper-to-bumper traffic all around Killarney Street, North Strand and all the way into town, so we took some back roads that led us to St Joseph's Mansions. There was a policeman there so we pulled down our window and told him that we needed to go down Sean MacDermott Street. *"I tell you what,"* he said. *"All the good-looking girls are going down Sean MacDermott Street tonight."*

Passing by St Joey's I said, *"Ma, go in and see the flats. You wouldn't know them."*

"Ah Jenna," she said, *"It's raining. I'm not going in now."*

"Go on," I said. *"They are absolutely gorgeous."* So I

drove her as near to the gates as I possibly could. Now the gates were completely different. They were electric with a security guard on duty. My ma said to him, *"I used to live here years ago. Would it be OK if I came in?"*

With that he opened the gate. I went in after her.

"Ma, what do you think? Aren't they gorgeous? You could be anywhere in the world. Would you like to live back here?"

"Jesus, Jenna, I don't really know because the balconies where we used to stand out and chat are gone. I preferred them the old way."

There was so much missing. First of all the playground and the balconies were gone and you couldn't go around the fours blocks on your bike, like we used to as kids, and you couldn't play our ball games against the pillars because they were missing. The most important memories of the flats were gone. I had grown up there in the 1970s and my ma had grown up in St Joseph's Mansions in the 1950s. Back then living in St Joseph's Mansion was like living on millionaires' row. Everyone wanted to live there and they were known as the posh flats. It was very hard to get into a flat unless you knew someone that was already living there. The old people lived on the ground floor and these were usually flats with one and two bedrooms. Larger families lived in the bigger flats and when their families grew up and moved out the flat would become too big and too much for an older person to manage. So sometimes the older family would swap their flat with the younger women and their family. This had to go through the corporation, of course, as it all had to be done legally. My ma says that people were very obliging.

Just like when I grew up in the 70s the playground opened at nine o'clock and closed at 1 o'clock for lunch and then reopened at 2.30 to 7 o'clock. The mothers were allowed to leave their babies down in the playground in their prams and the ladies would take care of them. Every Christmas a party was held for the kids and Santa Claus came and gave presents. Two men were employed to take care of the flats every day. They would wash the stairs of the four blocks, hose the chutes and clean out and disinfect them once a week. We could sense none of the St Joseph's of the 1950s or the 1970s there that day. We drove away and held onto our own memories.

THE END